The Theory and Practice of the Mandala

With Special Reference to the Modern Psychology of the Unconscious

Giuseppe Tucci

Translated from the Italian by
Alan Houghton Brodrick

DOVER PUBLICATIONS, INC.
Mineola, New York

Bibliographical Note

This Dover edition, first published in 2001, is an unabridged reprint of the work originally published by Rider & Company, London, in 1961.

Library of Congress Cataloging-in-Publication Data

Tucci, Giuseppe, 1894–
[Teoria e pratica del mandala. English]
The theory and practice of the mandala : with special reference to the modern psychology of the subconscious / Giuseppe Tucci ; translated from the Italian by Alan Houghton Brodrick.
p. cm.
Originally published: London : Rider, 1969.
ISBN 0-486-41607-0 (pbk.)
1. Mandala. 2. Subconsciousness. I. Title.

BL2015.M3 T83 2001
291.3'7–dc21

00-065620

Manufactured in the United States of America
Dover Publications, Inc., 31 East 2nd Street, Mineola, N.Y. 11501

CONTENTS

PREFACE

SOME readers may, perhaps, find this book rather too short, but I do not see what more I could say about Indo-Tibetan *maṇḍalas* and their meaning. My aim has been to reconstitute, in their essential outlines, the theory and practice of those psycho-cosmogrammata which may lead the neophyte, by revealing to him the secret play of the forces which operate in the universe and in us, on the way to the reintegration of consciousness. As is my custom, I have not dwelt too much on details—for then we should have become involved in unnecessary complications—but I have sought rather to give a brief summary of the intuitions and ideas from which the gnosis of the *maṇḍalas* stems. You will find in this gnosis some striking analogies with comparable ideas expressed by currents of thought in other countries and in other ages; and often real anticipations of modern and more structural theories. Things could hardly be otherwise, since we are dealing with archetypes which are innate in the soul of Man and which, therefore, reappear in different lands and at different epochs but with a similar aspect, whenever Man seeks to reconstruct that unity which the predominance of one or other of the features of his character has broken or threatens to demolish. I am not unaware of the researches of the psychoanalysts and especially of Dr. Jung, whose work seems to me to be destined to leave lasting traces on human thought.

Dealing with the *maṇḍala*, I have considered both the Buddhist as well as the Hindu *maṇḍala*; there may be difference in expression and designs, there may be a different accent laid on the psychological and theoretical situations, but, as a whole, the spiritual background is the same: the same is the yearning to find out a way from time to eternity, to help the primeval consciousness, which is fundamentally one, to recover its integrity. Philosophical trends may be several, but where we come to gnosis and the doctrine of salvation the gap is filled by the same desire of achieving liberation, of catching that instant, which once lived, redeems the Truth with us.

My desire has been to discuss the *maṇḍala* in such a way that I shall not misrepresent the opinions of the Indian Masters. In other words, I have been at pains not to lend to the ideas they express anything which might render those ideas incomprehensible to the men who formulated them. The theories of the *maṇḍala* took their origin in India and then penetrated into Tibet and these theories, expressed in symbols, allegories and connotations, have, as it were, the colour of the spiritual world in which they developed. So, I have endeavoured, rather, to place at the disposal of those who study the problems of the soul, new evidence concerning certain positions which, though they may be formulated in an original manner, are derived, all the same, from the inevitable and innate anxieties of the human spirit.

On the other hand, I hope that my attempt at being so objective or following so faithfully the Indian and Tibetan Masters will not be blamed. What I have wished to do is to allow the Indians or Tibetans to use their own language. What I have added may serve to put a little order into ideas which are often expressed in obscure and complicated phraseology that often may appear contradictory, and to extract their hidden meaning from the symbols in which they are enveloped. They are symbols which are well designed but also difficult to understand. Indeed, their original signification may today be unknown to the adepts themselves. So these symbols are uncertain and doubtful like writing in books to whose language we no longer possess the key. Still, they are symbols which, when we do learn to interpret them, share with the writers of the Upanishads the same noble aspiration: *Tamaso ma jyotir gamaya*—'Let me pass from the darkness to the light.'

I

THE DOCTRINAL BASIS OF THE MAṆḌALA

THE history of Indian religion may be defined as one of a toilsome attempt to attain autoconsciousness. Naturally, also, what can be said of religion applies to philosophy as might be expected in a country where religion and philosophy were blended together in the unity of a vision (*darśana*) that helps an experience (*sādhana*). In India the intellect has never prevailed to the extent of obtaining mastery over the faculties of the soul, of separating itself therefrom and thus of provoking that dangerous scission between the intellect and the psyche which is the cause of the distress from which the Western world suffers. The West, indeed, as though to designate its present inclinations, has coined a new word, unwonted in the history of human thought, the word 'intellectual'—as though it were possible to have a type of man reduced to pure intellect.

Pure intellect, indeed, detached from soul, is the death of Man. Intellect, self-confident and isolated in arrogant complacency, does not ennoble Man. It humiliates him, deprives him of his personality. It kills that loving participation in the life of things and creatures of which the soul, with its emotions and intuitions, is capable. Intellect, by itself alone, is dead and also deadly—a principle of disintegration. But in India intellect was never dissociated from soul. The world of the subconscious was never denied and rejected but, on the contrary, accepted and transfigured in a harmonious process intended to re-establish autoconsciousness, the consciousness of an Ego which is not, of course, the individual ego but *the* Ego, that cosmic Consciousness from which everything derives and to which everything returns. Pure consciousness, not darkened by a concrete thought, but, all the same, the premise of those concrete thoughts which make up the psychic reality of the living individual. Without that consciousness the individual psyche could not exist. But, on the other hand, the development of the psyche must be arrested if one wishes to reacquire, after the experience of life, the possession of that consciousness.

The Vedānta, the system of speculation which is derived from the Upanishads, calls this consciousness 'Brahman' and recognizes in us its mysterious presence as the *ātman*, the 'secret self', pure intelligence, First Principle, Sole Reality in the midst of the ocean of that which is in process of becoming.

The Śaiva Schools call it *Śiva* or *Parā-saṃvit*, 'Supreme Cognition' which is poured out and spread out in all that exists. Thus, in contradistinction to the monistic Vedānta, these Schools maintain that this world is not unreal but is the self-manifestation of God, that it is his garment. Error consists in attributing real, objective, autonomous existence to what appears as ego or a thing. Both ego and things are waves which, provoked by divine necessity and maintained by our error, arise and alternate on the originally motionless surface of that Consciousness.

Primitive Buddhism postulated the existence of two planes between which there is no communication, two worlds absolutely different the one from the other. On the one side, the world of *saṃsāra*, our own, in which *karma* operates and which is forever dying and being born again, and, on the other side, the plane of *nirvāṇa* reached by a qualitative 'leap' when *karma* and the force which causes it or derives from it are stopped or suppressed.

On this plane of *saṃsāra* the psycho-physical complex of Man is carried along in incessant movement. The conscious principle which is, then, the cause of moral responsibility (since by inspiring my actions it fashions my personality) projects itself, at the moment of death, into a new existence and predetermines it by virtue of the *karmic* experience which is accumulated in it and which is the cause both of the projective force and of my future character. But such predetermination is very comprehensive, inclusive of individual conditions in which is preserved completely the liberty of the individual; by being effected it exhausts itself.

It thus happens that although I suffer from my past, I remain always the free author of my future. Lives repeatedly develop, linked together like the rings of a chain, until cognition and experience (lived within us), that the universe is solely a becoming and a flux, arrest the course of *saṃsāra*. At that moment there occurs, as I have said, the 'leap' into *nirvāṇa*, which is beyond *karma* (*asaṃskṛta*). More than this, it is probable that early Buddhism did not say. But this proposition, with its schematic concision, could not fit in with the ontology that has always prevailed in Indian inquiry. It is an ontology which, finally, came to dominate Buddhism also. The plane of *nirvāṇa*, indeed, came, very early on, to be defined in ontological terms and was conceived as an Absolute, that is to say the premise of all phenomenal appearances which, while having in it their origin and their justification, suddenly flash on the surface of the sea of existence, to disappear rapidly, burned in the fire of gnosis. This was a conclusion arrived at in various stages. At one time it was affirmed that *saṃsāra* and *nirvāṇa*, thus contrasted, were equivalent inasmuch as they partake of the same character, since both are equally devoid of essence; the sole reality remaining is indefinable being. At other times this being was defined in positive terms as pure consciousness without object or subject. The world of appearances, or, as the Buddhists say, of duality, finds there its justification. Although this duality is not real, it cannot be said that it does not have a relative existence.

Let us take the oft quoted example of a man who sees a coil of rope in the dark. At first he thinks that he sees a snake and is therefore very alarmed. His fear is real and of the same intensity as it would be were he confronted with a real snake. However, as he draws closer he becomes aware that there is no snake at all, only a rope—and his fear disappears. It is of no consequence that his first perception was not 'real' since it induced in him the same feelings as if it had been 'real'. But his fear disappeared entirely as soon as he noticed that what he saw was a rope and not a snake. Thus, the plane of relative existence, from the point of view of the Absolute, has no consistence but may determine action. It is like a mirage. Such is the doctrine of Vijñānavāda. 'Relative consciousness', says Asaṅga, 'which creates unreal images, does exist, but duality, that is to say perception and the object perceived, does not exist in it in an absolute sense, that is, as really existing. In it is the Absolute as non-existence of duality, but this duality is in its turn an absolute.'

The Buddhists gave various names to this Cosmic Consciousness: Matrix of all the Buddhas (*Tathāgatagarbha*), Absolute Identity (*Tathatā*), Basis of All Things (*Dharmadhātu*), Thing-ness (*Dharmatā*). But some Schools, that of the Vijñānavādins, for instance, called it *Ālayavijñāna* or 'store-consciousness', that is to say they understood it as psychological reality, collective psyche in which individual experiences are deposited to reappear in a single flux. No act or thought is ever lost but is deposited in that universal psyche which, therefore, and implicitly, is not an immobile entity but an 'experience' continually being enriched. In it, past and present live together, form a fruitful and inexhaustible soil on which grows the plant of the individual, so that when it dies it lets fall into this soil the seeds which perpetuate the life-cycle. This was an intuition which Buddhism carried to the highest degree of formulation, but there are to be found analogous ideas in other systems. The Śaiva School of Kashmir, to name only one, maintains also that *karmic* experience is never lost until all creatures have been carried back into the Absolute Consciouness indentified with *Śiva*. Thus, even when the worlds at last are consumed in cosmic fire, the force of *karma*, the sum of individual experiences, acts as though thrust forward for the creation of a new universe. The latter, then, is not initiated *ex novo* but conforms itself according to the predispositions which survive destruction, so that it begins where the old world ends and inherits from it all its characters and possibilities.

Indian thought has, therefore, established two positions: a metaphysical conception which postulates an immutable and eternal reality to which is opposed the unreal flux of appearances which are always becoming; on the other hand, what we may call a psychological construction of the world which reduces everything to thoughts, their relations, but these, nevertheless, although ephemeral, are possible inasmuch as there exists a universal and collective force which provokes and preserves them. This Absolute Consciousness, matrix of all that becomes, this Conscious Being, the premise of all thought, was very often imagined as light. We experience it as an interior illumination that flashes before our eyes when concentration has removed us from the alluring appeal of external appearance—to which the senses yield—and has led us to look within ourselves. It is colourless, dazzling light. In the Upanishads it is the *ātman* which consists of an interior light (*antarjyotir-māyā*), it is that light with which the poet wished to merge himself. 'From the unreal, lead me to the real, from the darkness, lead me to the light.' (*Bṛhadāraṇyaka Upanishad*, I, iii, 28)

In Mahāyāna Buddhism it is defined as thought by nature luminous (*cittam prakṛtiprabhāsvaram*): in the state of *bardo*, that is in the period which accompanies and immediately follows on death, light flashes before the eyes of a dying man and in the consciousness of a dead man henceforth freed from the bonds of the body and hovering hesitant between liberation and rebirth. If the conscious principle of the person recognizes this light for what it is, that is Cosmic Consciousness, Absolute Being, the cycle of *saṃsāra* is then interrupted. But if the conscious principle of the deceased is troubled by the dazzling refulgence and withdraws, allowing itself to be seduced by more soft and coloured light, it will be reincarnated in the forms of existence which this latter light symbolizes, and thus will be precipitated anew into the cycle of births and rebirths.

'O son of noble family, thou, such a one, son of such ones, listen. Now to thee will appear the light of the Pure Absolute. Thou must recognize it, O son of noble family. At this moment thy intellect, by its immaculate essence, pure and without shadow of substance or quality, is the Absolute expressed in the symbol *Kun tu bzang mo*.

'As thy intellect is void, think that this void does not fade away, thy own intellect remaining clear without hindrance, pure and limpid; that intellect is the Buddha *Kun tu bzang mo*. The insubstantial void of thy intellect and thy clear and shining intellect are identical: this is the ideal body of the Buddha.

'This intellect of thine, which is identity between light and void, dwells in a great luminous mass. It is not born and it does not die. It is the Buddha *Od mi ạgyur*. It is enough that thou shouldest know this.

'When thou hast recognized thy intellect as being, by its pure essence, identical with the Buddha, this spontaneous vision of thy intelligence rests in the thought of the Buddha.

'This must be said three or seven times in a correct and clear voice. In this way, first of all (the dying man) remembers the instructions which serve to induce that recognition and which were, in his lifetime, imparted to him by the Master; secondly, he recognizes his own intelligence free (from all concrete thought) as identical with that light. Thirdly, in recognizing himself thus, he becomes conjoined with, and never to be separated from, the ideal body. Salvation is then certain.

'O son of noble family, in the moment when thy body and thy mind separate, thou wilt experience images of the ideal plane, pure, subtle, scintillating, luminous, through their own nature dazzling with a light which alarms like the mirage that appears shimmering on desert plains. Do not be frightened by these visions, have no fear for this is the constant play of the ideal plane's lightning which is within thee. Recognize it for such. By means of this light, the sound of the Absolute, with raging voice, will come like the roll of ten thousand thunder-claps which explode at the same moment. This is the sound of the ideal plane contained within thee. For that reason, be not afraid. Have no fear.

'Now that thou hast a mental body constituted by the propensities of thy *karma* and no longer a material body made up of blood and flesh, neither injury nor death can come to thee from that sound, from that light, from those flashes of lightning.

'Recognize these things only as thy own imaginings, recognize that all this is the intermediate state of existence.

'The world and its experiences are demolished. Then the images will appear like luminous bodies. The heaven will manifest itself as deep blue light. In that moment, from the depths of Paradise, T'ig le brdal, which is in the centre of the Universe, will appear the Blessed rNam par snang mdsad, white, seated upon the leonine throne. He holds in his upturned hands a wheel with eight spokes, and he clasps in his embrace Nammk'a dbyins "The Mother".

'A deep blue light, the manifestation of the gnosis of the sphere of ideas, the purification of the Conscious Principle, of deep blue light, transparent, emanating from the heart of rNam par snang mdsad and from the Mother in mutual embrace will appear to thee in such a way that thy eyes will not support it.

'Together with this (deep blue light) there will rise before thee the white light (emanating from) the world of the Gods and not dazzling, corresponding to the light of gnosis. In that moment, through the force of thy *karma*, thou wilt have fear, terror and dismay because of that deep blue light of gnosis of the sphere of ideas; it is as a splendour of dazzling lightning and thou wilt flee, and thou wilt feel born within thee a desire for that white light (emanating from the world of) the Gods, which is not dazzling.

'Therefore, have no fear, have no terror of that deep blue light of dazzling, terrible and awful splendour, since it is the light of the Supreme Way. This is the refulgence of the Tathāgatas, the gnosis of the sphere of ideas; but thou must have faith in it and intense devotion and must pray with fervour thinking that it is the refulgence of the compassion of the Blessed One rNam par snang mdsad. In him must thou take refuge and the Blessed One rNam par snang mdsad will come toward thee in the distress of the intermediate existence. This white light that does not dazzle is the Path of Light accumulated by thy mental perturbation. Have no attachment for it, have no desire for it. If thou have for it attachment thou wilt wander in the world of the Gods and transmigrate in the six different spheres of the intermediate existence and there will arise hindrance to the Way of Salvation. Therefore, turn away thy eyes from it, and have trust in that deep blue light of dazzling splendour.'

The Indians have not thought of life as a struggle between good and evil, between virtue and sin, but as an opposition between that Luminous Consciousness and its opposite, the psyche and the subconscious which they call *māyā*. All experience is a conflict between the intrusion of this *māyā* (which begins to operate with life itself, which is, indeed, life itself) and that conscious Being. The vital process tends fatally to the victory of *māyā*. *Māyā*, objectively, is the magical liberty which creates its own net around that light, darkens it and hides it. But it is not a force that emerges miraculously from nothing. It is born of the Cosmic Consciousness, in unity of the Primordial Consciousness which contains it within itself.

Between God and the world, between the Absolute and life, the conscious Being and the psyche, there is an unequivocal identity of nature; not an opposition but, as it were, a superposition of planes. Thus, Buddhist Schools affirm an essential identity (*aikarasya*) between pollution (*saṃkleśa*) and purification (*vyavadāna*), between *karma* impurity and purity which transcends *karma*; and there is an identity already present in the equivalence between *saṃsāra* and *nirvāṇa* to which I have alluded above. In the same way, Śivaism admits that in the indiscriminate brilliancy of the Cosmic Consciousness (in which originally 'I' and 'this' were the same), in the moment in which the intellective state (*vidyā*), by a spontaneous insurgency of *māyā*, succeeds the intuitive state (*sadvidyā*), there takes place in that primordial Unity a scission between subject and object. From this derives an autolimitation (*saṃkoca*) of God, by which we also (with our limitations and our vanity) are nevertheless that same God, although in a state of *aṇutva*, of almost molecular entity.

In fact, Divine Omniscience in which there was no Ego as opposed to a non-Ego—but only an absolute, eternal, unmoved Ego—becomes, because of *māyā*, clouded and darkened.

The infinite soul, as though lulled to sleep, thinks itself to be *puruṣa*, that is to say, limited consciousness. The attributes of this divine essence were five: eternity (*nityatva*), all-permeance (*vyāpakatva*), plenitude (*pūrṇatva*), omniscience (*sarvajñatva*), omnipotence (*sarvakartṛtva*). But now, by the operation of *māyā*, that Supreme Being projects itself as though distant from itself, as an object. It no longer recognizes that subject and object are indentical in its primordial unity, so that, forgetful of itself, it substitutes for that infinity five limitations. This eternity circumscribes itself in time (*kāla*), this all-permeance in determination (*niyati*), this plenitude in desire (*rāga*), this omniscience in intellect (*vidyā*), this omnipotence in limited creative capacity. Here then is constituted the individual Ego contained and hidden by these five sheaths (*kañcuka*) and opposed, as such, to the ultimate objectivization of consciousness; the *prakṛti*, nature, the non-Ego, matter from thinking matter or intellect (*buddhi*) to raw matter.

The Vedānta says the same thing. Once the process of limitation is effected by the spontaneous intervention of *māyā*, the obscuration of the Ego in the envelope of appearances (which hides the Ego and makes it appear manifold and diverse) developes in five stages. These are the five sheaths in which the Ego comes to be enclosed. Each sheath represents a different possibility of error, so that the inexperienced, the unawakened, take one or other of them as the Ego, which, however, is beyond and outside them. The first is the body, the sheath made of food (*annamayakoṣa*), since food is its nourishment; but the body is unstable and cannot, consequently be the *ātman*. The second sheath is that of *prāṇa* (*prāṇamayakoṣa*), of the vital force, which is quintuple, the five breaths which accompany life and which leave it at death. The third is the sheath of the mind (*manomayakoṣa*), that is, the psyche in all its complexity of volitions and ideas, the differentiation between the Ego and the non-Ego, the overflow of the passions. But not even this mutable and opposing flux of pleasant or painful states of mind can be the *ātman*. Indeed, until this tumult, which troubles the mind, is stilled, there can be no hope of attaining the liberating gnosis. Then follows, as the fourth sheath, that of the understanding, intellection (*vijñānamayakoṣa*). The Vedānta accepts, in its structure of the phenomenal world, a great deal of the Sānkhya conception. *Buddhi* is the foundation of the psyche, but, as in the Sānkhya, it is evolved from *natura naturans*; it is, therefore, nature, matter, ignorant in itself but appearing conscious because upon it falls the light of the intelligence, of the Ego. It is, indeed, precisely this reflection of the luminosity of the Ego on to *buddhi* which is called *jīva*, that is, the individual soul, the unique Ego, erroneously, by imposition of *māyā*, individualized as a particular ego: 'My own ego'. In this phase occurs contamination. The *ātman* is enveloped by *karma*, joins itself, in illusory fashion, with bodies, passes from existence to existence, suffers, and only in time of deep sleep, when no image moves or disturbs it, can it acquire once more its own peculiar untroubled serenity, transcending both pleasure and sorrow.

The spell will remain until gnosis has put an end to the imposition of *māyā*. Ignorance then disappears, like some magic apparition called up by a wizard. Suddenly all illusory appearance vanishes.

The fifth sheath is composed of beatitude (*ānandamayakoṣa*). Also the Supreme Consciousness, the *ātman*, is, by definition, beatitude. But in life are experienced reflections of the *ātman's* transcendent beatitude, as that which is produced in a state of profound sleep, undisturbed by emotions or by the memory of them. It is a beatitude which, likewise, may be attained in certain mystical conditions or in those of aesthetic contemplation. But as these do not last they cannot be the *ātman*. The Other is beyond even this last plane, outside this last sheath. Our perception of the soul, then, reduces itself to the perception of the *jīva*, the Ego individualized.

In virtue of this germinative presence of *māyā* in God,

our psyche, which is derived from its work, is bivalent. While it may disperse more and more into the negation oft hat light until it entirely obscures it, it may also, as though impelled by the glimmer that is not entirely extinguished in it, disengage itself from the night, discover once more our essential divinity, and induce us to find our way back along the path that leads to the plane beyond *māyā*.

This process, whose possibilities are mysteriously present in ourselves, develops as does the course of day and night. By day when the psyche spreads out into multiplicity, objectivity, duality, and thus disperses itself; or by night, when the object retreats, restored in its absolute and archetypal potentiality, in that consciousness which contains the ideas of all that will be, as the sixteenth segment of the moon (*tithi*) which, eternal and immutable, governs and stands above the alternating succession of the white and black fortnights.

From this it is clear how the anxiety of Indian gnosis is caused by an heroic attempt to withdraw oneself from the domination of *māyā* and to escape from the net in which *māyā* holds us captive and which we ourselves make the stronger by our ignorance of what we are. For, as Abhinavagupta says, ignorance (*ajñāna*) is twofold; the innate (*pauruṣa*), the autolimitation of God—the consequence of his voluntary decline in time and space; and intellective ignorance (*buddhigata*) increased by ourselves. 'Twofold is ignorance, the first intellective and the second innate. The first consists of uncertain and erroneous judgement; the second is nothing else but thought itself, (*vikalpa*) insofar as this is divine Consciousness in its limitation. As such, this is the principal cause of *saṃsāra*.' (Tantrasāra: p. 3)

Māyā, that is force objectively implicit in God himself, becomes, subjectively, *avidyā*, nescience, complacent abandonment to life, incapacity to raise the veil behind which, in the most profound depths of ourselves, reality lies hidden.

Māyā acts by its natural determination, moving from the very bosom of original Consciousness. But *avidyā* is contributed by individualization whereby the darkness becomes more dense and the light more distant.

Thus, owing to the operation of *māyā* and of *avidyā* there develops that space-time world (into which we are submerged) and also our own psyche, that is to say a duality which does not originate outside, but inside the Cosmic Consciousness (either Buddha or Śiva as one likes) by the upsurge within it of its *māyā* force.

This is, precisely, a magical liberty. It is the cause of *saṃsāra*, of life, of the process of objectivization and of personification. It is the many as opposed to the one, a centrifugal force by means of which this original Consciousness will end by sinking into the night of the unconscious, down, down until it becomes the negation of itself, materiality. It is the provisional opposition of an unconsciousness to that consciousness, an arbitrary creation of images. This magical force is *śakti*, 'power', the *dynamis* which creates the phantasms of existence. As such, *śakti* is feminine and, in fact, in the symbolism we shall deal with later on, it is represented in a female aspect.

These premises explain why India has not, apart from a few rare exceptions, awaited the advent of any saviour. Man is indeed consciousness lapsed in time and space, but liberation depends upon himself. There is no mediator who can save him. It may be objected that the Buddhas, or the manifestations of the Supreme Truth, which the followers of the Vaishnava Schools call *Avatāra*, help man to liberate himself, but such aid is generally afforded indirectly, since these beings teach the way of salvation. Salvation, however, must be accomplished by the individual, by his capacity to relive such teachings in himself. There is no grace which can modify the course of *karma*. A man inevitably reaps what he has sown. But in saying this, I do not wish to convey that the theory of grace is altogether unknown in India. Such an idea is present in Great Vehicle Buddhism too. Amidism in Japan is wholly centred upon an expectation of divine grace represented in the figure of *Amitābha* (Amida in Japanese). Likewise many Vaishnava Schools recommend a hopeful surrender in the arms of the omnipotent mercy of God.

But still, with the exception of these special Schools, men in India, if they would rediscover within themselves the divine spark, must rely upon themselves. They must draw out into the light the Supreme Reality hidden in themselves, and this they will be able to do only by recognizing it. And so, all the Indian systems proclaim the necessity for knowledge and initiation. We should, indeed, remember that the attitude of India—and therefore of the peoples who have been influenced by her thought—has tended, with time, to become initiatory. That is to say truth is a personal conquest which one attains through a mystery. It is a long and wearisome ascent during which, one by one, there must be cast aside the impediments, the obstacles, the veils which hide the truth so that, at last, the sought-for light may dawn. Except for a few special Schools which admit the operation of grace—or the 'divine touch' (*śaktipāta*)—God never shines in the human soul unless he is insistently invoked, almost constrained by violence.

'First of all desire of knowledge' is the usual phrase with which all Indian treatises begin. But this knowledge is not—and it is well to stress this point—dialectical, logical, discursive. Dialectical, logical, discursive knowledge is a necessary framework on which is constructed the instrument with which one works. Real knowledge, that which leads to cognition of ourselves and rebuilds the lost equilibrium, is experience, since knowledge to which action is not conformed is not a good, but an evil thing. When knowing does not transform life and is not realized in it, disharmony is caused. Knowledge may mature by initiation—called *abhiṣeka* or *dikṣā*, according to the School—which serves, as Abhinavagupta says, to expel innate ignorance, that is the limitations which obscure divine Consciousness. It completes, so to speak, the way of knowledge, by putting in motion, with its liturgies, psychological forces, by renewing, in the spiritual sense, him who seeks initiation, by causing the certainty of knowledge to pass into a permanent possession of most durable experience.

Just as Śaivaism affirms that we ourselves are of the same essence as Śiva, so also, some Mahāyāna texts and especially the Diamond Vehicle—which is the ultimate phase of the Great Vehicle—postulate an essential identity between the Buddhas and all creatures. In us is present the *Tathāgatagarbha*, the Seed of the Tathāgatas, and this is a fundamental assumption for the attainment of salvation. When two planes are essentially different, no passage is possible from the one to the other. Between two contrasting substances there is no contact. Only when essential identity exists (even if it be not perceived as long as we remain in the night of *māyā*) is palingenesis possible. This *Tathāgatagarbha* is the gem hidden in dross of which mention is made in the *Laṅkāvatāra*, one of the most authoritative texts of the Great Vehicle scriptures. It is, then, the *bodhicitta*, the thought of Illumination which is not only the goal of total reintegration but also the point of departure. It is our interior reality, a *logos spermatikos* which underlies everything and which we should find once more, luminous and splendid, in the midst of the darkness into which we have fallen.

Great Vehicle Buddhism (especially the Diamond Vehicle) and the Śaiva system constitute, then, a soteriology in which salvation is aimed at, that is to say the reintegration in us of that luminous Consciousness, present as *bodhicitta*, as *logos*, as Śiva, and this salvation is reached by means of an experience which involves all the life of the spirit and therefore produces a complete revulsion—or, if one wishes, reintegration. It should not be forgotten that everything, it is said, happens either through the psychical or the physical world, through space and time, through the cosmos and the Ego. The two planes, in these above-mentioned Schools, are superposed or interpenetrated, in the sense that the limitation of God in spatio-temporal manifestation is accompanied by a disintegration and an obscuring of his light. In the physical world involution is redemption, a progressive process of reabsorption and of disappearance into the immediately preceding state until the complete elimination of the plane of *māyā*. In the Ego the process is one of reintegration, of return to the original unity after the subconscious has been overcome, after possession has been taken of it through symbols. Reintegration is not possible without this experience, this living in the midst of the world of *māyā* and then dissolving it, annihilating it with that conscious experience, since to know by testing means to dissolve.

This reintegration develops by a revulsion (*parāvṛtti*) from the plane of *saṃsāra*. This is the *āśraya pāravṛtti* systematically set forth by Asaṅga and Vasubandhu but which had already been elaborated in the Schools before the time of these Masters. The word means 'revulsion of the prop'. The prop is the individual's psycho-physical complex, the apparent substratum, according to the Buddhist conception, of the human personality. 'The prop (*āśraya*) is the body furnished with the organs, that is the support of that which rests on it, that is of thought (*citta*) and of the mental states (*caitasika*)' (*Abhidharmakośa*, ed. La Vallée Poussin, III, p. 126). This prop is then the body which transmigrates and is exactly as it has been made in a given place and time, by the *karmic* imprints formed during past existences. It is provided with a thinking activity which appropriates it, inspiring new actions which, in their turn, determine the future destiny: rebirth and transfiguration.

This revulsion of the prop is understood by some Schools

in a matter-of-fact manner as a change of personality operated by *karma*, as in the case where a woman is reborn as a man, or a man becomes an animal (ibid., IV, p. 24, n.1). But in reality it is a total and absolute modification of the individual, the complete overcoming of the normal psychic plane, the realization of reintegration by the dawning of Illumination (*bodhi*) in the depths of our being.

It is in these words that Asaṅga and Sthiramati describe this central experience of Buddhism, an experience which defines and constitutes its soteriology:

'The state of Buddha in which, with various modes of complete abandon, the seed overcomes the moral and mental obstructions which from time immemorial follow us, signifies a new situation of the psycho-physical complex (*āśraya*) which is accompanied by sublime qualities of all the pure attributes. The attainment of this new fulfilment is brought about by following the most pure way of gnosis which aims at a great objective and is divorced from all imaginative process.

'There, as though standing upon a high mountain, the Tathāgata dominates the world with his gaze. He has pity on those who delight in serenity, how much more then upon other people who delight in existence!' (Asaṅga: Mahāyāna-sūtrālaṅkāra. IX, 12, 13)

'When knowledge perceives no object, it remains as pure knowledge since, as there is no one perceivable, it perceives nothing.' (Vasubandhu, *Triṃśikā*)

Comment:

'When knowledge does not perceive, does not see, does not grasp, it does not attach itself to any object existing outside thought, be it preaching, moral instruction or something of everyday experience such as form or sound etc. and that by the effect of a vision corresponding to the truth, not by reason of congenital blindness, then there is nothing more for knowledge to perceive. And then one discovers that (one has reached) the essential reality of one's own thought.' And the author explains the cause: when there is something perceptible, there is a perceiver, but when the perceptible is not there, that is to say when there does not exist a perceptible, there is implicit the non-existence of the perceiver, not only of the perception. Then arises a transcendent, homogeneous gnosis devoid of object and subject, in which all imagination is absent, and there disappear those imprints which cause us to be attached to the perceptible and to perception.

'When thought finds itself in this condition of pure knowledge how can it be designated?'

'In the ascetic there occurs a suspension of thought and an absence of perception. This is transcendent gnosis, revulsion of the prop caused by the suppression of the two sorts of twofold disequilibrum (*dauṣṭhulya*). This is the pure plane (*anāśraya*) transcending thought, the good, stable, blessed plane, the body of Liberation of the Buddha, called the Body of the Dharma.' (29, 30)

'In these two verses allusion is made to the perfection of results obtained by the ascetic who enters the way of pure knowledge, passing through a gradation of qualities ever higher and beginning with the "way of vision". Since percipient thought and a perceptible object no longer exist, he finds himself in a condition of suspension of the thought-function, of absence of perception. This is transcendent gnosis, that is supermundane, because in the world it is unusual; it has no purpose, since no creative imagination appears.

'Immediately after this gnosis, there occurs the revulsion of the prop; that is why he says "revulsion of the prop", which in this case is the psyche, in which the seed of all things is preserved. The revulsion of it is that which takes place when a quiescence (*nivṛtti*) is brought about, because all propensity (*vāsanā*) toward disequilibrium, karmic maturation or duality is absent, and, instead, there are present ductility (*karmaṇyatā*), the absolute body and the gnosis of non-duality.

'By the suppression of what is this revulsion attained? By the suppression of twofold disequilibrium, that is the disequilibrium caused by moral and intellective darkening.' (*Vijñaptimātratā-Triṃśikā* of Sthiramati, Triṃśikā, 29, 30)

This revulsion is threefold: let us consider the Buddha himself, since in him was accomplished the drama of which we have been spectators but in which it is possible for us to become actors, and so to reproduce in ourselves the events of his spiritual life.[1]

When a Bodhisattva sits upon the *bodhimaṇḍa*, that is to say on the Diamond Seat which is the ideal centre of the world and the plane of the Absolute, and attains the Illumination by which he becomes a Buddha, there is accomplished the first revulsion, for then the series of mental states which constituted his apparent personality is suppressed, all connection with the plane of *saṃsāra* is severed whether it be the result of former *karma* or the cause of new, future maturation. He has ascended to a metaphysical plane removed from all possibility of disturbance and change. He finds himself in a state of pure and crystalline brilliance, the sign of the 'leap' from the plane of *saṃsāra* to that of *nirvāṇa*.

In the second revulsion there is carried out the total assumption of a new, transcendent personality, which is mystical and manifests itself by a sort of reciprocal, mysterious substitution, to those creatures whose spiritual purity has caused them to ascend to superhuman planes, vulgarly called 'paradises', where, freed from the chains and

[1] For further details *vide* E. Lamotte *La somme du Grand Véhicule* (Louvain), p. 253 *et seq.*

limitations which bind us, they contemplate the immaculate refulgence of supramundane visions.

In the third revulsion is accomplished consubstantialization with the Absolute, beyond all irruption and predominance of the forces of *māyā*, beyond all visible form. Reintegration is then an accomplished fact.

2

THE MAṆḌALA AS A MEANS OF REINTEGRATION

THEORETICALLY, then, we may be able to reconstruct this process. But how can it ever come to and develop in the spirit of the initiate? In other words, what assistance does the neophyte seek in order to facilitate this revulsion? How can he dominate and overcome subconscious *māyā* in a return to the unity of consciousness? And how can he pass through the stormy and troubled sea of *māyā* in which he is shipwrecked? How can he bring back the plurity into which our psyche is shattered, to the *Bodhicitta* or Śiva, the One, Luminous, Undifferentiated Source?

Māyā, as we have seen, is an individualizing force, it personifies. Therein lies its strength, but also its weakness. *Māyā* assumes forms and figures by means of which contact may be established between it and consciousness and it may be, in this way, limited in its power. The cosmic process is expressed in images, pictorially. The successive phases by which the One, through dichotomy—duality, subject-object—splits into the multiplicity of things, or is darkened and clouded in the subconscious, are imagined in the forms of masculine or feminine deities, beatific and terrifying. Almost all these deities have been borrowed from the religious experience of the people. Often they are very ancient mythographies, which have survived among the lowest and least cultivated classes and which retain primitive and barbarous intuitions. Or again, such images have been purposely invented in order to express, with the efficacy which symbols have, the intricacy of the psychological forces underlying the multifarious movements of the world.

The neophyte can, in this way, grasp this unstable universe of powers which are both within him and without. For him the symbol is like a magical and irresistible admission into this formless and tumultuous tangle of forces. With the symbol he grasps, dominates and dissolves it. Through the symbol he gives form to the infinite possibilities lying in the depths of his subconscious, to inexpressed fears, to primordial impulses, to age-old passions.

But such a taking of possession can occur only when the neophyte knows how to interpret this symbology and not if he plunges therein at random. There is a way of arranging it so that it may become profitable and not slip out of our hands as though it were some precious instrument we did not know how to use.

We are just vaguely cognizant of a light in which we place our inner being; it shines like a spot of light on a moonless night. But how can we reach it? How can we return to it and lose ourselves in it?

In such circumstances was devised the scheme which represents, in complex and symbolical fashion, this drama of disintegration and reintegration; that is to say the *maṇḍala* in which the twofold process is expressed by means of symbols which, if they be wisely read by the initiate, will induce the liberating psychological experience.

It must not be imagined that the pictorial representation of the *maṇḍala* is peculiar to the Buddhists, who have, indeed, only given greater precision to the elaboration of a most ancient intuition which, with the passage of time, has become clarified and has also adopted some alien conceptions, at least as far as the exterior pattern is concerned.

This is not the place to discuss the origins of *maṇḍala* construction, of its meaning and sense, since in this book we are concerned not so much with the problem of origins as with the ideas of which the *maṇḍala* (as elaborated in the gnostic Schools of India and in the countries which have accepted Indian experience) has become the centre and the symbol. Therefore let us take these ideas at their full development and not at their starting-point.

First and foremost, a *maṇḍala* delineates a consecrated superficies and protects it from invasion by disintegrating forces symbolized in demoniacal cycles. But a *maṇḍala* is much more than just a consecrated area that must be kept pure for ritual and liturgical ends. It is, above all, a map of the cosmos. It is the whole universe in its essential plan, in its process of emanation and of reabsorption. The universe not only in its inert spatial expanse, but as temporal revolution and both as a vital process which develops from an essential Principle and rotates round a central axis, Mount Sumeru, the axis of the world on which the sky rests and which sinks its roots into the mysterious substratum. This is a conception common to all Asia and to which clarity and precision have been lent by the cosmographical ideas expressed in the Mesopotamian *zikurrats* and reflected in the plan of the Iranian rulers' imperial city, and thence in the ideal image of the palace of the *cakravartin*, the 'Universal Monarch' of Indian tradition. Such correspondences and theories, of Mesopotamian origin, accord well with primitive intuitions according to which the priest or magician marked out on the ground a sacred area. This, by the line of defence which circumscribes it, represents protection from the mysterious forces that menace the sacral purity of the spot or which threaten the psychical integrity of him who performs the ceremony; it also implies, by magical transposition, the world itself, so that when the magician or mystic stands in the centre he identifies himself with the forces that govern the universe and collects their thaumaturgical power within himself.

To this end, in ancient India, a vase was employed, a round receptacle which was not abandoned even when the theory of the *maṇḍala* was elaborated in all its details and in a definitive manner. Five vases, indeed, are placed in the five sectors of the *maṇḍala*, one in the middle, and one on each of the four sides. Each is filled with various substances. A vase remains an indispensable adjunct in all those Hindu ceremonies designed to bring down the divine essence (*āvahana*) so that it may be projected and take up its abode in a statue or other object. Such a 'descent' takes place, first of all, from the celestial plane into the vase and then passes through the channel of the sacrificer. Then, the small volume of the vase, or the small delimited surface, became, magically, the universe on which the magician or the mystic —identified with the supreme powers—operated according to the inviolable laws of the rite.

This construction of the world, this magical reflection of the universe, is also to be found in the exorcism liturgy of the Bon po, that is to say of the indigenous Tibetan religion. The Bon po Masters construct *mdos* or symbolical representations of the world. These *mdos* have four stands on each of which is a stick to which is fixed transversely another piece of wood so as to form a cross. Around are disposed images of the Gods. The exorcist identifies himself with the essence of these Gods, with the soul that revivifies the cosmos, whereby he transforms himself, ideally, into the principle of all that exists, so as to be able, when thus thaumaturgically omnipotent, to act as he pleases and to control the forces of the universe. The *mdos* is a world magically constructed and by transfiguration the world itself where the wizard is absolute lord.

The same concept of adaptation of a space to or of its conformity with the cosmos is one that, as I have said above, dictated the plan of royal palaces in the East. For these, according to the Mesopotamian scheme, represent the world rotating round an axis which is the throne of the king and is identified, ideally, with the central mountain of the universe or with the Pole Star, the immobile pivot on which all turns. And not only royal palaces but ordinary dwelling-places were, originally, a superficies transformed into a centre through which the *axis mundi* ran and so put the inhabitants into contact with the three spheres of existence, the subterranean, the median and the superior, that is to say, the inferior, the atmospheric and the celestial. This took place when the planes were ruptured by the axis of the world being magically transported into the dwelling. Thus in the tent of the shepherds of Central Asia, and certainly of the earliest Tibetans, the hole at the top through which the smoke passes corresponds with the 'orifice' of the sky, the Pole Star, in a cosmical system thought of as a gigantic tent.

Such then are the complex premises from which the *maṇḍala* derives. It is a geometric projection of the world reduced to an essential pattern. Implicitly it early assumed profound significance, because when the mystic identified himself with its centre, it transformed him and so determined the first conditions for the success of his work. It remained a paradigm of cosmic involution and evolution. Yet the man who used it no longer wanted only return to the centre of the universe. Dissatisfied with the experience of the psyche he longed for a state of concentration in order to find once more the unity of a secluded and undiverted consciousness, and to restore in himself the ideal principle of things. So the *maṇḍala* is no longer a cosmogram but a psychocosmogram, the scheme of disintegration from the One to the many and of reintegration from the many to the One, to that Absolute Consciousness, entire and luminous, which Yoga causes to shine once more in the depths of our being.

Experience then suggested certain analogies. Man places

in the centre of himself the recondite principle of life, the divine seed, the mysterious essence. He has the vague intuition of a light that burns within him and which spreads out and is diffused. In this light his whole personality is concentrated and it develops around that light.

The first Indian expression of this intuition (instinctively imagined in the form of a *maṇḍala* which has, in its centre, the luminous point of consciousness, like the hub of a wheel, from which stream forth the psychic faculties) is to be found in a passage of the *Bṛhad-āraṇyaka Upaniṣad* (II, 4, 15) which reads as follows: 'As all the spokes are connected both with the hub and with the rim, so all creatures, all Gods, all worlds, all organs are bound together in that soul.'

Long afterwards a Tantric text repeats: 'Then imagine that all the spokes assume the aspect of the Goddess: as eternally the rays shine forth from the sun, thus also the Goddesses arise from the body of the Great 'Goddess.' (*Gandharvatantra* quoted in *Śāktānandataraṅginī* p. 137)

In like manner the deities of the *bardo* are always present in the disposition of the *maṇḍalas*:

'O son of noble family, there will appear to thee a light of four colours, the symbol of the purification of the four elements. In that moment, from the paradise called T'ig le brdal which is in the centre of space, will appear to thee the Buddha rNam par snang mdsad, father and mother, as on the first day. From the paradise called mNgon pa dga' which is in the east, will appear to thee the Buddha rDorje sems dpa', father and mother with their acolytes: from the paradise called dPal dan Idan, which is in the south, will appear to thee the Buddha Rin c'en hbyung Idan, father and mother with their acolytes; from the paradise Padma rtsegs dbe ba can which is in the west there will appear to thee the Buddha sNang ba mt'a' yas, father and mother, with their acolytes; from the paradise called Rab rdsogs which is in the north, there will appear to thee the Buddha Don yod grub pa, father and mother with their acolytes.

'These will appear to thee in a luminous rainbow. O son of noble family, in addition to the circle of the five mystical families, there will appear to thee the four irate deities, guardians of the doors, rNam par rgyal ba and gŠin rie gshed and the King rTa mgrin and bDud rtsi hk'yil ba and the four female deities, guardians of the doors, lCags kyu ma, Zabs pa ma, lCags sgro ma and Dril bu ma and the six blessed Buddhas, he of the Gods, brGya byin, he of the demons, T'ag bzang ris, he of men, Škya seng ge, he of the world of the animals, Seng ge rab brtan, he of the ghosts, K'a hbar ma, he of the hells, C'os kyi rgyal po. And also there will appear Kun tu bzang po and Ku tun bzang mo, father and mother, ancestors of all the Gods. Also the deities of the plane of intelligible forms, emanating from thy own heart, will appear before thee. These thou must recognize as images simply emanating from thyself. O son of noble family, these paradises also are not situated elsewhere, they are disposed in the centre and at the four cardinal points of thy heart and coming forth from it they appear before thee. These shapes come from no other place; they are solely the fabric of thy mind. As such thou must recognize them. O son of noble family, these images are neither large nor small, they are of just measure, each one has its own proper ornaments, is seated in its particular posture, has its own throne, and its hands are held in the gesture appropriate to it. These images are permeated (with the essence) of the five couples and each one of the five symbols is surrounded with a halo of five lights.'

A usual representation of this interior *maṇḍala* vision is a flower—properly speaking, the lotus. Its four or eight petals disposed symmetrically about the corolla symbolize the spatial emanation of the One to the many. In India, the lotus has been regarded as expressing a twofold symbolism, which may be called exoteric and esoteric. The first denotes creation in its widest sense, generated from the primordial seed of the cosmic waters, as in the myth of Brahma rising from the navel of Nārāyaṇa lying upon those waters. The lotus is the earth itself on those same waters (*Taittirīya-Saṃhitā* Sv. p. 1, 3c), and the prop of the universe. (Śayana R.V. VI, p. 16, 13)

The second meaning of the lotus which has dominated the millennia of Indian religious experience is a spiritual one, the symbol of the other plane which reveals itself in the centre of the mysterious space (*ākāśa*) in the depths of the heart. (*Chāndogya Upaniṣad*, VII, 3 I)

The first creation is in space and time, the second starts from this limitation but, by transcending the process of becoming, accomplishes (through contemplation) that qualitative 'leap' by means of which the spirit of the meditator finds itself transported into a different and more exalted sphere.

The lotus is the sign of palingenesis because the new spiritual state takes its origin in the depths of the heart, in that secret recess which the heart encloses just as at the origin of creation God, manifesting himself, filled the infinity of space with his emanation and his progressive unfolding. In that lotus, in the secret of the heart, is the mysterious presence of the Absolute, the *puruṣa*.

'This uncreated great *ātman* is, among the vital spirits, the depositary of consciousness; in the space that is within the heart lies the Lord of All, the Ruler of the Universe, the King of the Universe.' (*Bṛhad-āraṇyaka Upaniṣad*, IV, 4, 22)

'Verily like unto the extent of space is the void within the heart. Heaven and earth are in it. Agni and Vāyu, the sun and the moon, likewise also the stars and lightning and all other things which exist in the universe and all that which does not exist, all exists in that void.' (*Chāndogya Upaniṣad*, VIII, 1, 8)

In the space of the heart, magically transfigured into cosmic space, there takes place the rediscovery of our interior reality, of that immaculate principle which is out of our reach, but from which is derived—in its illusory and transcendent appearance—all that is in process of becoming. This rediscovery, naturally, is accomplished by degrees. Transfiguration from the plane of *saṃsāra* to that of *nirvāṇa* occurs in successive phases, by degrees; just as on the cosmic mountain and around the *axis mundi* are disposed, rank after rank, one above the other, the Gods ever purer. Little by little one rises towards the peak and beyond the peak right up to that summit of all that becomes and has form (*bhūta-koṭi*), where takes place the passage to the other plane.

And these degrees, according to well-known Indian tradition, are symbolized by images of the Gods. Thus is visualized the process of reintegration from the many to the One and it is accomplished in a twofold manner. It may happen that the meditator, by suitable means, so acts as to force the divine plane (symbolized by a particular deity) to descend into him. This is the violent evocation of a mystical state, *avāhana*, or in some Schools *samāveṣā*, the state of being possessed by the deity and thus symbolically, the descent of a God into the midst of the heart and by which the meditator is transfigured. This descent produces in him a change of plane. He is identified with the spiritual plane symbolized by this same God. This contact produces a deification. The veil of *māyā* is rent and destroyed. This is the deification necessary in the liturgical ceremonies which prescribe that no one who has not himself become God may be able to adore God: *nādevo devam arcayet.*

Or else it is an inverse process, that is to say the meditator evokes, from the infinite possibilities of consciousness mysteriously present in his own heart, the divinity with whom he desires to identify himself. He evokes this divinity according to the traditional prescriptions of Yoga. Each deity has his own mystical essence expressed by syllabic symbols which constitute his mysterious principle. For the meditator, who imagines this luminous and flaming seed in his heart, and who at the same time concentrates mentally on the aspect of the God as shown in the traditional pictures, this syllable, flaming from the fire of gnosis, gives rise to the particular image which he receives in the centre of his heart. Thus, in the motionless Cosmic Consciousness, as soon as the first differentiation occurred, there arose the archetypes of the following creation. However, some formulae of meditation and evocation will be found more useful than my explanation. When these formulae are compared with one another they will be found to throw light upon each other and to make clear the phrases of this spiritual process. The first evocation is concentrated on Caṇḍamahāroṣaṇa and the other on Tārā.

'The mystic sits down in such a way as to feel no discomfort and in a place which he finds suitable. Then he must think of the solar (that is red) *maṇḍala* placed upon a lotus-flower of eight petals in the midst of his own heart. There arises the syllable HŪṂ black in colour. The rays of light which stream from it will attract into the space in the middle of his heart the Buddhas, Bodhisattvas and Caṇḍamahāroṣaṇa of whom, farther on, mention will be made. After having paid honour to them, the mystic should confess his sins and then, in conformity with the rules of disipline, he should take the threefold refuge. He should rejoice in the good accomplished by creatures, offer himself as a ransom for the evil done by others and vow to attain supreme Illumination. He should meditate on the four pure types of behaviour (*brahmavihāra*), sympathy, pity, joy in the virtue of others and equanimity. He should realize that this world has no nature of its own, being deprived of subject and object, and he should meditate upon the absolute void repeating (the following formula): "In my adamantine pure essence is knowledge of the void." Then on the solar *maṇḍala* laid upon a lotus-flower of eight petals and situated, in its turn, on the plane of immaculate ether, he should think of the syllable HŪṂ as placed on the hilt of a sword which itself issues from a syllable HŪṂ of black colour. The rays which stream from it attract all the Buddhas and cause them to enter into the syllable HŪṂ. Then he should meditate on Śrīcaṇḍamahāroṣaṇa as though issued from that syllable HŪṂ.

'Then he should imagine that the sword—whose centre is marked by the letter HŪṂ born of the lotus and the sun in the heart of Mahākrodhācala—becomes transformed so that within the heart a second Caṇḍamahāroṣaṇa appears born of the syllable HŪṂ. But also in the heart of this last he should imagine a straight black sword marked with the syllable HŪṂ which is on the lotus and on the sun. The rays of light emitted from it should attract the *jñānasattva*, and he, looking at it as the *samayasattva*,[1] should attract it towards himself with the syllable *jaḥ*. Having washed out his mouth and sprinkled it with lustral water, he should make the *samayasattva* enter there (into the heart), bind it with the letter VAṂ, and satisfy it with the letter HOḤ; like water in water, he should consider the God as one with him.' (*Sādhanamālā*. Baroda, 1925, Vol. I. p. 173)

In the same way we read elsewhere: 'First of all the *yogin* should, for his concentration, enter a cell made agreeable with flowers of pleasing perfume, sit without feeling discomfort, and meditate that the letter A is transformed into a lunar (white) *maṇḍala* in which there is the seed TAṂ of yellow colour. He should see then the chorus of the *gods*

[1] On these two terms and what they signify see *infra* p. 96.

as though led in space before him by the luminous rays which emanate from that seed. He should honour with flowers etc. this chorus projecting from himself the Goddess Puṣpā (flower) etc. emitted by the respective essential formulae (bīja=seeds) placed in his own heart. Then to this chorus of Gods he should confess his own sins (saying): "I confess all my sins, I rejoice in the good accomplished by all the Buddhas, Bodhisattvas, saints and laymen, and I devote all the good I have done to the attainment of supreme Illumination. I take refuge in the Buddha, the most exalted of all men; I take refuge in the Law, the Great Vehicle in its entirety, and I take refuge in the assembly of Bodhisattvas who can no more lapse from the spiritual plane they have attained. May I reach supreme Illumination so that all creatures may derive from it benefit, advantage and welfare until they are able to repose in the absolute *nirvāṇa* in the illumination of the Buddhas. I entrust myself to the Way that leads to Supreme Illumination, which Way is the Diamond Vehicle."

'He should read the verses about this threefold refuge and then rouse by meditation the sympathy that brings happiness to all, the compassion that removes sorrow, the joy that is indissolubly bound up with divine bliss and the equanimity which cures moral infection. He should thus reflect upon (the nature) of things. All that (appears) is merely thought, which fallaciously appears as this or that species. As happens in sleep, there exists nothing outside thought, as an object. Since, then, no external object exists there is not thought as the subject of that object. Therefore all things are merely thought and their real nature is this ultimate Reality, void of object and subject. When he has appreciated this, he should eliminate all forms of things since they are only a sign of the error by which they exist, and he should understand that the sole nature of all things can be qualified only as absolute identity, similar to pure crystal, as the clear autumnal sky at midday.

'This is what is called knowledge of the absolute void that is transcendent beyond all efflux and all imaginative thought. He should fix this intuition with a *mantra* such as: "OṂ, my adamantine essence is knowledge of the absolute void. This is the perfection of gnosis. This is my supreme defence." Then, he should actuate by meditation the defence constituted by common knowledge in its pure aspect, derived from that absolute plane, and which has assumed a form. He should imagine that, before him, from the letter R the sun appears and in this sun, the *viśvavajra*[1] issued from the syllable HŪṂ. He should then imagine that this *viśvavajra* is transformed into a bastion and a cage of diamond: the rays that spread from the *viśvavajra* are hardly endurable, they are like the fire which burns the worlds at the end of the cosmic ages, they spread out in all directions, they consolidate forming a square bastion of flaming diamond. Above this is a cage of diamond, and below it a pavement of diamond down to the depths of the earth.

'Then sun and diamond project rays which spread through the quarters[2] of space and then consolidating in the outer gate, form the threshold. In the middle is a triangle called "Origin of Things" and essenced by the Great Vajradhara, white and pure like autumnal light. With its base above it terminates in a point upwards. Within it is space and in the middle a double lotus in whose pericarp

[1] By *viśvavajra* is meant '*double vajra*'. A *vajra* (in Tibertan rdorje—pronounced dorje) is a bronze or brass instrument employed in various initiatory ceremonies. By its shape it suggests the thunderbolt brandished by Jupiter. *Vajra* signifies both 'thunderbolt' and 'diamond' but the latter meaning is the usual one and it indicates precisely the indefectibility of gnosis and the intangibility of the Divine Essence. The *vajra*, when used in ceremonies, is joined with the bell, the latter is then considered as the symbol of the 'void', of the insubstantiality of all that appears and thus, by extension, of gnosis.

The *vajra*, then, is the symbol of the means (*upāya*) which, when united with gnosis, brings about palingenesis, that is of pity. In the rite, the *vajra* is inserted into the bell, which is held in the left hand, so as to indicate that the thought of illumination (*bodhi*), the essence we should resuscitate in ourselves, can be born only by the synthesis of the two poles; gnosis-pity. The *viśvavajra*, or double *vajra*, has the form of a cross.

[2] Four quarters, four intermediate quarters zenith and nadir.

lies a *viśvavajra*. On this altar are the four elements in the form of four *maṇḍalas* essenced by the four deities, one above the other. Then from the syllable YAṂ forms the *maṇḍala* which corresponds to the wind in the form of a bow and of grey colour and marked on the two extremities by two pennants; from the syllable RAṂ, that of fire, triangular and red, marked in the corners with the letter R; from the syllable VAṂ, that of water, round, white, marked with a bell and from the letter LAṂ, the *maṇḍala* of the earth, square, yellow and marked in the corners with a three-pointed *vajra*. Upon this is a wheel derived from the syllable BHRŪṂ. This is the symbol of transcendent knowledge which pervades all. Then, from the transformation of the four great elements, on the *viśvavajra* in the middle of the altar, arises a palace which represents, in synthesis, the pure kingdom of the Buddhas, the city of the Great Liberation, co-essenced by Vairocana.

'Square, with four doors, ornamented with eight columns, surrounded by four verandas, embellished with four arches . . . in the midst of it he should imagine the moon, born by transformation from a double row of vowels, and above this, a *vajra* born by the transformation of the syllable TĀṂ. On its border is another TĀṂ. From this the sun is born by the transformation of a double row of the following letters, ḌA, ḌHA, DA, DHA, YA, LA.

'When these two (sun and moon) are joined together, great bliss results. With the rays emanating from these seeds (that is the above-mentioned syllables) he may attract beings. Then, when he has caused the cycle of his protecting deities to penetrate (into himself) the *Yogin* should actuate by meditation the Goddess *Tārā*, born of the transmutation of these indicative syllables.' (*Sādhanamālā*, I, p. 224)

These two processes thus described are often merged together. In both the God who is evoked or who descends is visualized in the centre of the lotus-flower miraculously arisen in the space within the heart. This space is then changed by meditation or magic into primordial space, into the very point where the ideal history of the Universe eternally develops. In this process the Ego and God coincide in seminal synthesis and the illusions of time, space and the individual psyche disappear.

These two descriptions of the evocative process which occurs in the lotus of the heart have been taken from Buddhist texts because they are so detailed and minute. We should not, however, think that the system is peculiar to the Buddhists, for we are dealing with methods of mediation and evocation which are admitted by all the Indian Schools and on which these Schools base their own experiments intended, precisely, to draw forth from people in the world, the New Man, the *Puruṣa*, cosmic, absolute and infinite.

According to a Jain text,[1] the *Tattvārthasāradīpikā*, the meditator should imagine, in order to concentrate on it, a great motionless ocean of milk, in the middle of which he visualizes a lotus-flower as large as the *Jambudvīpa*, the southern of the four major continents which in Indian cosmogony make up the universe. This lotus has a thousand golden petals and its pericap rises up like a mountain of gold. The meditator should think of himself as seated on a throne on the peak of this mountain and as completely master of his passions. He is, so to say, transported, ideally, on to the peak of existence where he must work to free himself from *karma* so that he can 'leap' on to the plane of *nirvāṇa* and attain *kaivalya*, the final freeing of the soul from the impurity of *karma*, in virtue of which it regains its pre-*saṃsāra* purity.

In the second phase he imagines a lotus of sixteen petals level with his own navel. On these petals are inscribed fourteen vowels, A, Ā, I, Ī, U, Ū, E, AI, O, AU, Ṛ, Ṝ,

[1] Jainism is one of the most ancient religions of India. It still flourishes and the Jains recognize as their master the Jina Mahāvīra.

L, Ḷ plus AṂ and AḤ. The word ARHAN (a title given to the saint who has attained that isolation) now shines in the middle of the pericarp. Smoke will issue from the R of the word ARHAN (because R is the seed of fire), followed by sparks, and then a violent and uninterrupted flame which blazes and will burn a lotus of eight petals in the centre of the heart. This lotus symbolizes the eight species of *karma* which force the soul to transmigrate and prevent it from remaining isolated in its purity.

In the third phase the meditator imagines a whirlwind which disperses the ashes of this burned lotus.

In the fourth phase he must think of rain falling very heavily and cleansing his body of those ashes. Then he sees himself, finally purified, seated upon a throne and adored by a chorus of Gods.

We might give an interminable number of examples but they would be monotonous variations on one fundamental idea. The descriptions we have just given of these evocations in the form of *maṇḍalas,* allow us, instead, to make a very important observation.

The representation of the divine cycles in the form of a *maṇḍala* is not the result of arbitrary construction, but the reflection in appropriate paradigms of personal intuitions. By an almost innate power the human spirit translates into visual terms the eternal contrast between the essential luminosity of its consciousness and the forces which obscure it. From this process cognition is acquired.

When, for instance, we find in the pages of the *Bar do*[1] the divine lotus delineated, or in books on *Yoga* descriptions of the divinities evoked acting on the mystic flower in the midst of the heart, it is not a case of simple reflections from the *maṇḍala* scheme whose iconography has been elaborated by the different Schools. In other words the theory of the *maṇḍala*—diligently defined by the initiatory Schools—has

[1] The Tibetan Book of the Dead, translated by Evans Wentz into English.

not conferred this disposition on the divine choirs. It is just the reverse.

Such visions and flashing apparitions occur through some mysterious intrinsic necessity of the human spirit. It is to Jung's honour that he was the first to recognize this.[1] And such visions assume definite forms with rays, flowers, round and square patterns about a luminous central fountain. Men, by introspection, discovered these things and by reflecting on them, and then by combining them with cosmological conceptions, fixed their pattern in regular paradigms. Rules were defined and classifications established with the subtlety proper to theological Schools. Measurements and colours were prescribed. It was sought to contain the spontaneity of these images and visions within certain limits.

The *maṇḍala* born, thus, of an interior impulse became, in its turn, a support for meditation, an external instrument to provoke and procure such visions in quiet concentration and meditation. The intuitions which, at first, shone capricious and unpredictable are projected outside the mystic who, by concentrating his mind upon them, rediscovers the way to reach his secret reality.

We have, then, come to the point where we must describe a *maṇḍala*. We will divide it up into its different parts, and will seek, at the same time, to identify the various sources of the elements which have gone to make up its symbology.

A *maṇḍala* is drawn upon the ground on a purified surface consecrated with appropriate rites. Powders of different colours are generally used to trace the lines and draw the figures. The choice of colour is, of course, determined by the particular sector on which the figures are to be traced and according to certain correspondences of which we shall speak later. This is the rule followed in the case of the

[1] See Jung and Wilhelm: *The Golden Flower*.

maṇḍalas prescribed for the initiations into various Tantric cycles, that is admissions to the mysteries of esoterism whose truth is experienced in the depth of the spirit.

In later times *maṇḍalas* were also drawn on cloth so that the mind might be concentrated on their paradigms and thus visualize the construction of the world exposed in the various systems of salvation proposed by the Tantras.

The drawing of a *maṇḍala* is not a simple matter. It is a rite which concerns a palingenesis of the individual and in whose details this individual must participate with all the attention demanded by the importance of the result to be obtained. An error, an oversight, an omission render the whole operation useless. And this not because (as in all magical and ritual acts) precision in word and deed guarantees success, but because any defect is a sign of inattention on the part of the consecrator and indicates that he is not working with due concentration and absorption. So, there would be lacking the psychological conditions by which, in his spirit, the process of redemption is produced. All this explains why the Buddhist Masters have discussed, with great minuteness, the rules to be followed in making a *maṇḍala*. These begin with, for instance, the testing of the quality of the thread or fine cord to be used for tracing out the various parts; then we are told of how many twisted strands the thread should be composed. There should be five of them, each of a different colour. Such a thread, dipped in coloured powder, is indispensable for marking out the different parts of the *maṇḍala*. When the thread has been laid out on the surface where the *maṇḍala* is to be, the ends are held so that it is taut, then by raising it up and letting it fall suddenly, the powder in which it has been immersed makes a straight line. By repeating this several times, according to the diagram, there are obtained the schematic outlines within which the successive designs are marked. The treatises also lay down the measurements of this cord and what purificatory rites must be performed for the various implements which are used in the whole ritual act. There is no particular which is not described with minute care, as anyone who wants further information may see by reading, for instance, the treatise which Tsong K'a pa (the celebrated reformer of Tibetan Buddhism and founder of the Yellow Cap Sect in the fourteenth century) wrote on Vajrayāna.

In a general way, it may be said that a *maṇḍala* contains an outer enclosure and one or more concentric circles which, in their turn, enclose the figure of a square cut by transversal lines. These start from the centre and reach to the four corners so that the surface is divided up into four triangles. In the centre and in the middle of each triangle five circles contain emblems or figures of divinities.

We shall speak, shortly, of the symbolism of the various parts, but, first, we must state that on to this paradigm of essential lines is superposed a much more complex diagram—in which each of the component parts has not only its significance but a particular name. To make the explanation clearer it would be as well to refer to Plate No. 1, which, although reduced to its essentials, still shows how complex is the design of a *maṇḍala*.

A *maṇḍala*, then, is surrounded and circumscribed by a circle on which is displayed an uninterrupted line of scroll-work. This is the Mountain of Fire (*me ri*), a flaming barrier which, it would seem, forbids access, but which, in fact, according to the symbology of Tantric gnosis, represents consciousness that must burn ignorance, dispelling the darkness of error and leading us to that cognition which we are seeking.

Immediately after this circle a girdle of diamond (*rdorje ra ba*) is drawn. The diamond symbolizes Supreme Cognition, *bodhi*, Illumination, Absolute Essence, Cosmic Consciousness, which, once it has been attained is never again lost. It is, like a diamond, unchangeable. The Buddha, indeed, is seated upon a diamond and Bodhgaya, the place where he attained to Supreme Illumination and became the Buddha, is called the 'Diamond Seat' (vajrāsana). But this 'Diamond Seat' is not localized in any point in space, neither did Illumination occur just once under the *ficus indica* tree on that celebrated night when the Bodhisattva, after having discomfited *Māra*, the God of Love and Death who reigns over *māyā*, rose by degrees to the supreme Revelation and became the Buddha. The Diamond Seat is outside time and space, it is in every place and at every instant when there is a revulsion from this to the other plane.

Lapis-lazuli as well as a diamond is a symbol of the other plane. Indeed, the ground of the paradises of Amitābha or Amitāyus, the God of Light and Infinite Life, is of lapis-lazuli, being level and smooth, precisely because it is outside the earth and its limitations. For it is the realization of a spiritual condition in which there is no longer any movement or whirlwind of passion but only the clear and motionless brilliance of consciousness reconquered.

Then comes (especially in the *maṇḍalas* dedicated to the terrifying divinities) a circle in which eight graveyards are represented. In exoteric tradition these are eight awe-inspiring places where in various parts of India ascetics retire to meditate. They are disposed in a cross, like the diagram of the *maṇḍala*, four on the principal and four on the intermediate points. They are not nine, for there is no central point. They are peripheral, disposed on the outside limits of the *maṇḍala*'s cross-pieces or of the eight-petalled lotus which corresponds to the plane of spiritual essences. The central point is lacking because, esoterically, these graveyards do not correspond to definite places but symbolize the eight aspects of the individual and individuating cognition which has been lost. The individual is shipwrecked in the world of experience, is overwhelmed by the impact of his *karma* and has fallen into the power of the unconscious. There are eight aspects, because five are in contact with the five sensory consciousnesses, that is to say they correspond to the impressions which, through our senses, the external world communicates to us. Then come the intellective consciousness (*manovijñāna*), the thinking faculty of the individual, in itself and by itself (*vijñāna*), and lastly, the store-consciousness (*ālayavijñāna*), which gathers together and retains both individual and collective experiences.

These eight forms of consciousness (*vijñāna*) are the cause of *saṃsāra* and they condition its development. As long as they are active we are dragged along on the round of births and deaths. The graveyards symbolizing the *vijñāna* are represented according to a detailed iconographical plan. Each has its own mountain, its own *stūpa*, river, tree and ascetic who sits there absorbed and confident.

As can be seen, such a representation is analogous to that of the paradises. As the graveyards cover the space in the eight quarters, the paradises are placed, according to tradition, in the various cardinal points, even if some of them have caused the others to be forgotten or prevented them from rising to the first plane.

The paradises also have their trees, not the dreary guardians of cremation grounds, but glittering with gems and precious stones. Rivers and lakes enliven them with cool and perfumed waters. There are *stūpas* since these are the 'Body of the Law' (*dharmakāya*), eternal verity expressed in architectonic structure. The resemblances could be extended to many other particulars. What does all this mean? That *vijñāna* or *citta*, the Conscious Principle, mental experience or psychic activity is bivalent. It throws people into the billows of the ocean of existence, but at the same time it is an instrument, which, by annihilating itself, raises them, in a spiritual palingenesis, to the other plane, holding them attached to life and therefore to death, since whosoever lives, also dies, or else it transports them into the spheres where there is no more either life or death because they are beyond time. *Vijñāna*, like *śakti*, is bivalent. When symbolized by a triangle with its point downwards it is multiplication, disintegration; when by a triangle with its point upwards it represents the *kuṇḍalinī* awakened, tending toward reintegration in the primordial unity of Śiva, the *Śaktiman*, 'that which contains the *śakti* in itself', as indissoluble identity. We are confronted with the same ideas but expressed in a different language or with different accent.

Then the bones which whiten in the graveyards are read in a different fashion. They are the world seen and overcome, the terrestrial plane eliminated, seen from above as dead and dormant.

The initiate is for ever redeemed from it.

After the graveyards come a girdle of lotus leaves to signify spiritual rebirth—according to the symbolism mentioned above. The lotus leaves open outwards because the plane they represent is not brought to an end, but stretches out as it were towards the neophyte who knows the mysteries of gnosis and has relived them in his soul. The Gods, however, are seated upon a closed lotus, because they manifest themselves only upon the other plane whose essence they represent. They are at the journey's end. The outside petals turned outwards signify the entrance into the life of palingenesis, but the central bud of the lotus, closed upon itself, symbolizes the Original Synthesis.

In the middle of this first circle is drawn the *maṇḍala* properly speaking, which is also called the 'palace' (*vimāna*, in Tibetan *žal yas k'ang*), that is the place where the images of the Gods are disposed. Its proportions are determined by a unit of measurement that corresponds, generally, to an eighth of the *brahmarekhā*, that is of the line which bisects the *maṇḍala* from north to south and symbolizes the *axis mundi*, Sumeru, the spinal column of man, assimilated to the macrocosm. The unit of measurement for the minor figures is the fourth part of this segment.

In the middle of each of the four sides a gate opens in the form of a T, flanked with seven bands of five colours which are prolonged along the four sides, thus joining gate to gate and constituting the walls of this sacred city. Over the gates rises a *toraṇa*, a sort of triumphal arch, resting upon two, or more, lateral pillars. This *toraṇa* is composed of eleven little roofs, one upon the other and each shorter than the last. On the top of this arch is a disk on which is represented the twelve-spoked Wheel of the Law. To the right and the left, two gazelles recall the preaching of the Buddha's first sermon in the deer park at Sarnath. On the wheel is an umbrella, insignia of royalty, and at its sides are ornamental streamers in vases.

The walls, which as we have seen are represented by five strips of different colours, are called respectively 'base', 'border', 'bean', 'necklace', and 'half-necklace', since these two latter bands are decorated with necklaces either hanging down or issuing from the mouths of marine monsters (*makara*)—and finally there is the jewelled fringe. They are all surmounted by a balcony decorated with lotus flowers and on it Trees of Paradise rise up from vases containing the Water of Immortality (*bum pa bzang po bhadrakalaśa*). There are also seven gems, symbols of the Universal Monarch, a *Cakravartin*, that is the wheel with eight spokes, an elephant with six tusks, a green horse, a sixteen-year-old girl, a gem from which shine forth six rays, a red-coloured minister who holds a treasure in his hands and a black general with breast-plate, shield and lance.

The symbolism is clear, both in its origins and in its signification. It is derived, by a long road, from the Mesopotamian *zikkurat*, which was also a cosmogram of the universe, with at first five and later on for astrological reasons seven terraces.

Buddhism kept to the quinary scheme because this lies at the base of the cosmical and psychical dichotomy of Indian tradition. So, naturally, in the design of *maṇḍalas* the five walls are represented as strips of one and the same band, close together, but not for reasons of perspective one after the other. In any case, the correspondence between the groundplan of the royal city and the basic pattern of a *maṇḍala*, together with the emblems which decorate it, leave no doubt that the *maṇḍala* was thought of as a palace. This came about because of the relations between royalty and the sacred world ever since the dawn of Indian civilization. Śakva, the King of the Gods, sits on his throne in heaven, surrounded by his Court like an earthly king. His paradise is a great palace conceived on the plan of terrestrial palaces although fancy runs riot in describing its supramundane magnificence. In Buddhism this relation is still more marked, since onto the mystical figure of the Buddha has been superposed the myth of the *Cakravartin*, the 'Universal Monarch', conceptions which the Indians developed, progressively, as the vicissitudes of history brought them into contact with Iran and made them familiar with the imperial conceptions of the Persians.

The ceremony which is performed in a *maṇḍala* is, above all, an *abhiśeka*, that is a 'coronation' so called because it demands, as does the ceremony of a royal coronation, a baptism or aspersion with water. The figures of the Buddha shown on a *maṇḍala* often wear mantles and royal tiaras. The paradises of the different Buddhas are known as *Buddhakṣetra*, that is 'kingdoms of Buddha'. As soon as the baptismal ceremony has been performed, the disciple who enters into a *maṇḍala* is in some rituals invested with royal insignia and emblems. One of the baptisms is known as *mukutābhiṣeka*, the 'baptism of the tiara', because the neophyte, when his head has been encircled with a crown, must become a king, raised up above all the play of cosmic and psychic forces, and reintegrated with the Origin of all things. He is the king of everything, consubstantial with the Tathāgata.

The *maṇḍala* is represented within this ideal city. It is, properly speaking, the symbolical portrayal of offered gnosis, and is protected by another chain of *vajras* and circumscribed by lotus petals. Here is the place of the essential deities of the *maṇḍala* and of their symbols.

What we have briefly described above is the scheme or plan of *maṇḍalas* in Tibetan documentation which is the richest in pictorial examples of compact mystical diagrams. Here, also, the Tibetans have followed scrupulously Indian precepts and models. It is enough to read, in the different Tantras, the sections devoted to *maṇḍalas*, to realize that the Tibetan pictures conform—with a care that admits of no freedom or deviation—to the iconography described so minutely in the esoteric literature of India. Still, although the examples on which we have mainly relied (and which we shall soon describe) are all inspired by Buddhism, that does not mean the other religious schools of India do not know *maṇḍalas*.

Indeed, much use of them is made in Hinduism, for instance in the Śaiva School of Kashmir (and fully described by Abhinavagupta in his *Tantrāloka*). Here they have various forms and are intended to awaken the consciousness of our identity with the Universal Consciousness (*Tantrasāra* of Abhinavagupta, Chapters 14 ff.). They may be of two kinds, according as to whether they are intended to bestow special powers or lead to liberation, when the disciple is unified with the Lord. What is peculiar to this School is that the initiation in the *maṇḍala* may be conferred also to a disciple who is absent, or even dead (ibid., Chapter 16). In Hinduism, however, *yantras*, purely linear designs expressing the same principles, are usually substituted for *maṇḍalas.* In nearly all of them the place of the deities' figures is taken by the corresponding *mantras* which express the mystical essence in a symbolism of sounds, by complex combinations of different-sized triangles, or by the lotus flower on whose petals are written the mystical syllables. It is clear then that a *yantra* represents, in its essential plan, the linear paradigm of a *maṇḍala.*

All this has come about owing to the uncompromising attitude and almost aversion from self-revelation which invaded the Śiva and *Śākta* mysteriosophical Schools of medieval India. These were disinclined to show images of the deities to non-initiates. Furthermore, the Śaiva and *Śākta* pantheon is not as rich as the Buddhist and is not, like the latter, set within the framework of a rigorously defined theophany. The *śakti* or 'powers' mentioned by the Hinduist Schools—in addition to the Supreme *Śakti,* identified with Kalī, Durgā or Pārvatī capable of appearing in innumerable manifestations—are vague, from the iconographical point of view often indeterminate and, thus, very different from the deities of Buddhism in which each divinity was represented in an aspect which was easily identifiable as his own, since he was provided with definite symbols and given a precise relation to various spiritual planes.

The best example of a Hinduist *maṇḍala* is that called *Śrīcakra*—'The Wheel of *Śrī*', that is of the *śakti,* or divine power which is the motive force of the universe and by virtue of which God manifests and displays himself in things which are all, of necessity, the effect of *śakti* itself, since without it the God can do nothing. 'Only conjoined with thee, O Śakti,' says the *Saundaryalaharī,* 'have I the power to be Absolute Lord, otherwise God would not even be able to move' (strophe I). It will be enough to note—without going into details of the construction—that such *maṇḍalas* are made by four isosceles triangles with the apices upwards, and by five others with the apices downwards; they are of various sizes and they intersect one another. In the middle is a point, the *bindu*, the mysterious matrix. (Plate 3)

These triangles are circumscribed by a first circle on which are drawn eight petals which symbolize the mystical lotus of creation (which we have mentioned above); then follows another circle with sixteen petals; after that a three-fold circular 'girdle' (*trimekhalā*) fitted into a square with—as in a *maṇḍala*—four openings towards the four cardinal points (*bhūpura*). In this complex of triangles which serve to show the refraction of the original *Śakti* in some fundamental aspects, the five downward, facing triangles indicate the quintuple aspect of the *Śakti*, while the four with apices upwards symbolize Śiva. However, other authors, such as Lakṣmīkara, read in the opposite way, that is to say, as though the five triangles indicative of the *Śakti* had their apices upwards. But the difference is merely apparent, it depends, that is to say, on the phase on which the initiate fixes his attention. The downward-directed apices of the *Śakti* triangles are symbols of the tendency to fulfilment, while when they are turned upwards they indicate the contrary phase, that is the return.

As may be seen, in this *maṇḍala* there is no image of any divinity. There is no iconographical representation. Everything is reduced to a geometric design complicated by multiple intersections of the same figures. The only thing which remains from the Buddhist *maṇḍala* is the outer 'girdle' with the gates—and also the lotus flower. Line is substituted for image. However, the principle remains the same. What we have, in fact, is the quintessential reduction of an identical idea.[1]

Except in its greater linear simplicity the *yantra*, indeed,

[1] A *maṇḍala* of the Devī is described in detail by Bhāskara Rāya in his commentary on *Vāmakeśvara Tantrāntargata nityaṣodaśikarnava* (Ānandāsrama S. S., p. 36 ff.); this chapter written by the famous Tantric teacher is very important for the theory of Hindu *maṇḍalas*.

does not differ from the *maṇḍala.* The meaning and the use of both are the same, and both may be provisional or permanent. The *yantra* may be drawn when it is necessary and then it may be destroyed or erased, or, on the other hand, it may be lasting. Of the latter sort are the *yantras* inscribed on stone or bronze which are often to be seen in Hindu temples.

The initiatory ceremonies which are performed with *yantras* make use, almost always, of that primitive symbol of the *mundus* which is a vase filled with pure, perfumed water containing various ingredients and placed in the centre of the *yantra*, since it is there that the descent of the deity takes place.

3

THE SYMBOLISM OF THE MAṆḌALA AND OF ITS VARIOUS PARTS

Now we know the basic plan of the *maṇḍala*. We have, so to speak, reconstructed its skeleton. We have described the scheme of lines which composes it, which divides it into parts, and cuts it into sections. However, all this is but the exterior diagram. Now we must see what is to be drawn upon its surface and what may be the symbolical significance of the figures that should be designed thereon, and, above all, we must consider how the initiate must read this tangle of hieroglyphics and how, through these images, he may ascend to the hidden meaning which they typify.

A *maṇḍala*, as we have seen, is divided into five sections, while on the four sides of a central image, or symbol, are disposed, at each of the cardinal points, four other images or symbols. We should, however, guard against understanding this division in the primitive or cosmographical sense. In a *maṇḍala* the quinary grouping of images and symbols is psychologically significant as well as indicating the four cardinal points that revolve round a centre[1] which conditions them, thereby evolving a succession in time and space round itself. A *maṇḍala* is, indeed, the All as reflected in the ego. The five points marked on it correspond to the five structural elements of the human personality, centred on the

[1] The *askaram padam*, the undecaying condition. *Guhyasamāja*, p. 90.

conscious principle, the kernel of the individual, the cause of *saṃsāra* and also of the Return.

The macrocosm corresponds to the microcosm, but in esoteric symbology the latter prevails over the former; not indeed as a physical prop, but as a psychical complex, since it is the revulsion of the psyche and nothing else which is, in fact, to be accomplished. Naturally intervention remains. The whole perceptible world was in Hindu speculation divided into quinary groups. On this conception the Sāṅkhya constructed the scheme of its categories which is still the framework of all the Schools' dogmatics: the five elements in subtle or coarse state, the five colours, the five objects of the senses, the five senses themselves.

Then this quinary division is projected from the external into the internal world.

According to the Buddhism of the Diamond Vehicle original consciousness, symbolized by Mahāvairocana, Vajradhara, Vajrasattva or Akṣobhya, is radiated into the Five Buddhas: Vairocana, 'The Brilliant One'; Akṣobhya, 'The Unshakable'; Ratnasaṃbhava, 'The Matrix of the Jewel'; Amitābha, 'The Infinite Light' and Amoghasiddhi, 'The Infallible Realization'.

Likewise, Paramaśiva, the Supreme Śiva, that is Pure Consciousness, assumes five faces of different colours from which derive the five directions which correspond to the five 'families' of the Buddhist Schools, White Sadyojāta to the West, Yellow Vāmadeva to the North, Black Aghora to the South, Red Tatpuruṣa to the East, all grouped around the central face which is that of the Green Iśāna. From these faces emanate the initiatory revelations which—like the 'families' of the Diamond Vehicle—divide creatures into groups each one of which has its own irreducible capacity and, therefore, can be reintegrated only by the particular way which is suitable to it. The actions which are suitable to the western and southern revelations are those proper to the *paśu*, that is the 'herd', creatures of inferior intellectual and moral level. To the western revelation are suited only the works of the herd and 'heroic' ones (*paśu* and *vīra*)—by 'heroic' being meant those who practise Yoga. Divine and heroic works correspond to the northern revelation and divine are those which overcome the plane. To the central revelation only divine works are suited. Thus, we see that the Śaiva Schools divide men into three classes: first the common people, those who live a herd-like life, for whom precise laws and prohibitions are suited, since such men do not yet possess a consciousness which can, by itself, govern itself. Then come 'heroes' who have a tendency to emerge from such a night. But their capacity wearies them. They follow their own consciousness and make their own laws, different from and contrary to those of the herd. They are lonely men who swim against the current; courageously they put themselves into contact with God and free themselves from the uniform life of association. Then come the *divya*, the holy souls, who are fully realized and so beyond the plane of *saṃsāra*.

In many Schools of Buddhism the correspondence between macrocosm and microcosm is expressed in other terms. The five Buddhas do not remain remote divine forms in distant heavens, but descend into us. I am the cosmos and the Buddhas are in myself. In me is the cosmic light, a mysterious presence, even if it be obscured by error. But these five Buddhas are nevertheless in me, they are the five constituents of the human personality.

It is the same intuition which underlies the building five layers of bricks in the vedic altar homologous to Prajāpati and by which the sacrificer recovers his own identity with Prajāpati himself; in the same way the presence in man of the five breaths presided over by the five gods, sun, moon, fire, rain and wind, reproduce in the microcosm the synthesis of the macrocosm.

Buddhism has taught from the beginning that this personality is an aggregate of five constituents. There is no metaphysical entity which is always identical to itself and which survives death. There is only a body, made up of five elements, and a psyche which, in each one of us, preserves the individual and collective predispositions of the past and enriches them with its own peculiar experience. I am *rūpa*, that is, 'form' which represents the physical prop, so to speak, of my individuality; I am *vedanā* or sensations, insofar as I collect the perceptions of the world which my senses yield me; I am *saṃjñā*, 'notion' or 'discrimination' of things; I am *saṃskāra*, that is the force, or coefficient of *karma*; in my past and future life my 'I' has never been standing alone, but only in relation to others; therefore *karma* resumes in itself, as I have said, the individual and collective experience which I bear in me from my birth and which forms the psychological ground on which develops my real personality, but *karma* is, at the same time, the propensity of my future; I am *vijñāna*, particular and individual knowledge, and then, following on that, consciousness, the centre of moral responsibility, the capacity to decide on action, to dominate the *saṃskāra*, to arrest it and so to transfigure it that it may no longer become a force propelling to a new existence, but may die away, thus producing the essential conditions for the 'leap' on to the *nirvāṇa* plane.

But in our personalities there is also something else. There is emotive life in which lie dormant, but ready to burst forth, the five passions or fundamental obscurations, that is to say mental darkness (*moha*), pride (*abhimāna*), jealousy (*īrśā*), irascibility (*krodha*) and cupidity (*lobha*).[1] When the original identity has disintegrated, emotive life rises up in all its forms and errors, with an equivalence dominated by the scheme of the five colours according to the following diagram:

[1] See *Guhyasamāja*, pp. 5 ff. and Fig. 1.

Buddha	*Colour*	*Components of the Personality*	*Passions or Perturbations*
Vairocana	White	Matter	Darkness
Ratnasaṃbhava	Yellow	Sensation	Pride
Amitābha	Red	Notion	Concupiscence
Amoghavajra	Green	*Karma* Coefficients	Jealousy
Akṣobhya	Dark Blue	Cognizance	Wrath

In fact, light and shade, consciousness and passion, good and evil are irreparably intertwined in man. With life he accepts his destiny of struggle. His task is to counter-balance the two worlds as represented in the symbology of the *maṇḍala*. God and Goddess are embraced on the same throne. If one should prevail over the other the *maṇḍala* would lose the symmetry of its parts, the psychical life of man would be perturbed and salvation, the Return, be precluded. For this reason Buddhism never speaks of the 'repression' but of the 'transfiguration' of these passions, since they are, in fact, essential elements of our psyche. Any attempt to suppress them would provoke their more violent and inflexible reawakening. Therefore not their suppression is required but their transfiguration or rather their transference whereby consciousness itself is enriched. The original struggle is soothed into a harmony which prepares the way for return to Primordial Unity, in Primeval Equilibrium. However, these passions and emotions which constitute, as it were, the waves of our psychic life, and which clash and rise high, result from the contact between the ego and the world, from our reaction to the environment which presses in upon us from all sides and forces us to give heed to its voice and its summons. The individual is involved in active participation in the life of things and reacts in various ways. The psyche is enriched, perturbed and moved by an uninterrupted exchange with the outer world. The essential duality of the individual—consciousness and perception—is expressed symbolically by the representation of each of the five Buddhas accompanied by a *mudrā* or counterpart. These latter are Locanā, Māmakī, Pāṇḍaravāsinī, Tārā and again Māmakī. They are also called Rūpavajrī, Śabdavajrī, Gandhavajrī and Sparśavajrī, that is the perceptions of sight, sound, smell, taste and touch, but in their diamond (*vajra*), that is essential, form.

In Buddhism, as in most of the Śaiva Schools, all this occurs by emanation from the Unique Principle of Cosmic Consciousness. But in the Śākta Schools—which give pre-eminence to *māyā*—the world is the work of *māyā* alone, the active force of God, and which, as the cause of divine multiplication, acquires superiority. Having assumed all the characters of the *prakṛti*, the *natura naturans* of the Sāṅkhya system, *māyā* spreads out over all that exists, while God, the Absolute Soul, one or multiple—when imprisoned in the illusory individuality of *māyā*—remains inert, taking colour, like a crystal, from the reflections projected on to him by the passions with which *māyā* is stained. For this reason, in Buddhist iconography, the mother (*yum* in Tibetan) is represented embraced by an active and dancing God, where as in the Śākta Schools the positions are reversed. The God is inert and the *śakti* is active. In some cases he lies supine like a corpse while the *śakti* performs on his body a frenzied dance to the rhythmical movement of whose steps the worlds are born and die.

With the exception of this difference of posture there is one unitary conception which extends from Buddhism of the Diamond Vehicle to the Tantric Schools of Hinduism. The whole drama of the universe is repeated in ourselves.

The *maṇḍala*, which represents consciousness shining forth in a quintuple series and is expressed in the pictures of the Buddhist sects, has not been as popular in the religious art of the other Indian Schools. Yet, their dogmatics are not far removed from this same premise. A comparison with the doctrines of the Śaiva Schools, although revealing a diversity of conception with regard to details, brings out the essential identity of the ideals. These Schools, also, recognize (although arbitrarily since diversity cannot be admitted in the One) a Supreme Aspect, *Paramaśiva*, which, like the Buddhist *Vajradhara*, is the extraspatial point, the zenith from which all things develop and are conditioned, from which—in order that it may be understood, let us say —are projected five modes of being, called *tattva* or 'categories':

1. The *Śivatattva*, that is pure consciousness, the absolute ego.

2. The *Śaktitattva*, as closely linked with the first as the rays that accompany light; it is the being that indissolubly accompanies the ego, absolute concreteness anterior to the cognition that is expressed in the phrase 'I am'.

3. The *Sadāśivatattva* is the cognition of this being without, however, any scission between subject and object: 'I am' and 'I am This', that is the same ego anterior to all the archetypes in the universe.

4. The *Īśvaratattva*, the 'This' is brought about while the cognitive aspect is accentuated; no more 'I am This' but 'This am I', the stress, that is, lies on the archetype.

5. The *Sadvidyā*, is always expressed in the formula 'I am This', but the 'I' and the 'This' are perfectly balanced and although identical in essence, they anticipate diversity; this is what is termed by the Indians 'diversity in unity' (*bhedābheda*). It is a quinary scission which takes place on the plane of the Absolute and which naturally is not developed in time but is effected in an eternal contemporaneity where, only metaphorically, can we separate and distinguish this phase and isolate it from the Absolute Being, *Paramaśiva*, in whom all exists and becomes.

However, in this quinary series the same *maṇḍala* paradigm is found which the Buddhists express in their pictures and which is reflected in the five gnoses of which the five Tathāgatas are the symbols:

Akṣobhya, *dharmadhātujñāna*, coincidence of knowledge with the Absolute Being, Primordial Consciousness identical with the One Being.

Vairocana, *ādarśajñāna*, knowledge in which, as in a mirror, the archetypes of things are reflected.

Ratnasambhava, *samatājñāna*, knowledge of the fundamental identity of things in that all are fleeting images emanated from that depth.

Amitābha, *pratyavekśājñāna*, knowledge in virtue of which the Sole Being appears as this or that.

Amoghavajra, *kriyānusthānajñāna*, knowledge through which power is expressed as act and spreads out from it.

But it is possible to push the analogy still farther. God is indistinguishable from his interior power, which assumes an infinite number of aspects and modes, but which always remains the same inexhaustible force (*akṣara*) which moves everything and by virtue of which God creates, acts and commands. This divine activity presents five main aspects which are: *cit-śakti* or intelligence, *ānanda-śakti* or beatitude, *icchā-śakti* or will, *jñāna-śakti* or consciousness and *kriyā-śakti* or activity.

Each one of these aspects is, in its turn, linked with one of the five modes of Śiva (to which I have alluded above) so that we have—without forgetting that duality is the inevitable effect of our limited means of expression by which we are obliged to enumerate as distinct phases what are indissoluble in the primordial identity of the Being—the following aspects:

Śiva-tattva	*cit-śakti*	intelligence
Śakti-tattva	*ānanda-śakti*	beatitude
Sadāśiva-tattva	*icchā-śakti*	will
Iśvara-tattva	*jñāna-śakti*	consciousness
Sadvidyā	*kriya-śakti*	activity

Let us now translate this ontological construction either into the symbolism of the *maṇḍala* which expresses—with the aid of visible designs—the modes of the divine Being, or into myself, for besides my ephemeral, illusory identity, I am essentially that same essence. The result is something which is none other than a *maṇḍala* analogous to that of the Buddhists. The five Gods, all on the same plane, each one embraced with his own *śakti*, or (in Buddhism) mother, while, ideally, there rises above them the omnipresent and all-pervading Zenith, Paramaśiva, or the Buddhist Vajradhara, in whom they are eternally present. The only difference we can note is the predominance given, in the Śaiva Schools, to the *śaktis*, whereas it is the masculine aspect which prevails in Buddhism. But, if we discount this difference in stress, we shall find in both cases the same metaphysical construction and the same quinary scheme which serves to express it.

Thus the One, the Primordial Consciousness, spreads itself out, becomes actuated, scattering its light into the opacity of the psyche, and there rests in a wavering refraction which appears as other than itself. Nevertheless, in such scattering not all consciousness is extinguished. It is markedly limited, it is as though imprisoned in darkness, attracted and repulsed by an object, circumscribed in duality, but it is not extinguished. In Buddhism, from the five Buddhas come forth groups of Bodhisattvas, that is creatures whose essence is *bodhi*, of that primordial brilliance to the reintegration of which we tend after the experience of the world. The Bodhisattvas are luminous constellations grouped round the Buddha himself. They are the compassionate, succouring companions of Man, ever ready to hasten to his call. According to hagiographical traditions, the Bodhisattvas, incalculable eons ago, vowed to reach illumination so that they might aid other creatures in this struggle against pain and illusion to escape from the cycle of *saṃsāra*. Thus, symbolically, is expressed the active value of consciousness when it is not completely dimmed and destroyed by disintegration. The *logos spermatikos*, that is *bodhi*, is the necessary premise of our reintegration, since if it did not exist we should have no possibility of issuing from the chaos into which we are plunged.

The human person, then, it is worth repeating, is a co-existence of two opposing tendencies, the one centrifugal and the other centripetal, thus, as the one tendency leads us out of ourselves, the other guides us towards the return, towards the central point, the undecaying condition (*akṣaraṃ padam*).

We are, then, following the development of the psyche and of the cosmos from the primordial centre in its infinite expansion and radiation. We are proceeding, in this teaching, from the invisible point which stands above and determines the development of the *maṇḍala*. Then, we see the pentad undergoing another scission owing to the arising of corresponding forces, and hence we behold the manifestation of the pentad of Bodhisattvas whose presence is a necessary condition for our salvation. But the process goes on.

We have now reached the periphery from which the four gates open on to the four cardinal points. These are gates facing towards all that lies outside our consciousness, that consciousness which is beyond our control (but which is accessible through figurations and representations), always rioting about in a dark, confused struggle. Generally, these gates are protected by some guardian of terrifying aspect.

Such fearsome figures are therefore called the 'custodians of the gates'. Armed, awe-inspiring and monstrous in appearance, they keep watch, either alone or accompanied by their female counterpart with whom they dance frenzied dances.

Who are these demons to be found on the edges of the *maṇḍalas* and who are almost always present at the entrance of those architectonic *maṇḍalas* called temples? According to the usual terminology such beings are named the *vighnāntaka*, that is 'those who put an end to *vighna*'. *Vighna* are 'impediments'. By 'impediments' is understood, in Tantric gnosis, those forces which menace the sacral purity of the places where the rites are performed, and also those forces which are obscurely present within us and hamper our journey towards the light. They are demons, but their iconography is not so precise and so particularized as that of the 'terrible' deities. Only a few of the demons are represented in a well-defined iconographical scheme. They are just *vighna*—in the plural—a confused and indistinct mass, whirling about in the depths of the subconscious ready to burst forth at the first occasion so as to possess themselves of the psyche and to agitate it with their disturbance. They are obscure and almost invisible in the darkness that submerges them. Their supreme ruler is Yama, the God of Death who is mounted on a buffalo and wields a club that is the spinal column of a huge skeleton topped with a human skill. Yama's head is that of a buffalo, horned, with flaming eyes, and his mouth drips blood.

As Death, Yama is *saṃsāra*, the eternal cycle of being born and dying, of the plane of life whose fruits are pain and sorrow. But, according to an ancient correspondence, he is also Kāma, love, because love and death are linked together, the one nourishes the other. How can consciousness struggle against these forces? By assuming a suitable form. The first struggle between light and darkness, says the teaching of Yoga—and the Buddhists repeat it—is not fought out in the fullness of consciousness. Consciousness could take no hold on the fluid and mysterious world of the subconscious. There is no possibility of contact between the two. If they touch they overlap. The unconscious may overflow into the conscious and suffocate it, extinguish it, but the conscious has no such power of eliminating and dispersing the unconscious. It is a matter of a long and difficult struggle that never ceases and which consciousness must carry right into the enemy's camp. This is possible in only one way, by assuming a pugnacious and terrifying appearance suited to the powers which must be combated.

As a result each of the deities of the superior plane emits from himself a *krodha*, that is to say a terrifying (*rudra*) emanation, a 'wrathful' one, which, symbolized in monstrous forms, represents the violent ingress of conscious forces into the shadows of the unconscious so as to cut at the root of the rival, or decompose it and to lead it, submissive and docile, towards the realms of light.

Such is the significance of the 'terrible' deities placed to watch over the *maṇḍalas* and to repulse the confused swarms of the mysterious world from which the dangers of the unseen burst forth, and, at last, to dominate them.

Therefore, these guardians have not only a defensive part to play but also an offensive one. They stand at the threshold of the conscious so that they may enter the other kingdom and take up their positions there, after they have, as I have said, assumed a form which makes them able to cope with the forces they must overcome.

Naturally, we do not imply that figures of divinities are always represented on *maṇḍalas*. In many *maṇḍalas* there are no representations of Gods but merely symbols or letters. However, the significance is the same in both cases, since, as is said in the *Yamala* (quoted from the śākta *ānandatar-aṅgiṇī*, p. 55), 'twofold is the aspect of Divinity, one, subtle, represented by the *mantra* and the other coarse, represented by an image'.

The syllable is, we may recall, the secret essence or 'seed' of the Divinity. The latter is so intimately bound up with the former that it is enough to concentrate one's thought upon it, for the image to be called up in one's mind. But no evocation occurs unless the mystical syllable has been, for a long time, meditated upon and visualized. This happens because in the gnostic symbology of India—and not only of

India—cosmic evolution and its reabsorption in the primordial matrix are reproduced according to a precise and subtle alphabetic scheme which,[1] in its combinations, reflects the weaving of the universal Becoming and determines, so to say, its various phases.

This explains why the *mantra* has so great an importance in the Indian liturgies. These 'seeds', which apparently have no meaning, present in the symbol of sound the correlation between the various planes and reflect the play of cosmic forces. Whosoever understands the complication of the 'seeds' acquires a mysterious power. But it is of no use to repeat the sounds mechanically without understanding their secret power. Of course, a sound is not, again, conceivable with its support, *prāṇa*, cosmic energy, the universal breath of many aspects and of infinite repercussions, *prāṇa* which represents the hidden life of God and of things. Every sound, by virtue of *prāṇa*, is inserted into the complex of powers (*śaktis*: in Buddhism *dākinīs*) by reason of which the One spreads out in the world, and reproduces in an essential paradigm its eternal and infinite combinations. In order to make what has been said more clear, it may be fitting to see how one of the many esoteric systems—for example the Śaivism of Kashmir—symbolizes, by means of vowels, the various phases of cosmic expansion.

'Cognition (by virtue of which consciousness becomes cognizant of itself and of things) is not an hypothesis. It is the embryo of the supreme sound identical with the very essence of consciousness. And it is cognizant of all the union of *śaktis*, of the powers of God which bring about the universe in all its extension. The principal powers of God are three: the supreme power (*anuttara*), will (*icchā*) and expan-

[1] See on this the above quoted commentary of Bhāskara Rāya on the *Vāmakeśvara tantra*, and chiefly the *Varivasyā-rahasya* of the same author, Adyar Library Series No. 28 and Abhinavagupta's *Tantrasāra*, now translated into Italian by R. Gnoli, *Essenza dei Tantra*, Torino, 1960. Introduction, Cfr. also J. Woodroffe (A. Avalon), *The Garland of Letters*, Madras, 1951.

sion (*unmeṣa*). This triple aspect of cognition is symbolized by the three vowels A—I—U. From this triad proceeds the diffusion of all the powers. Beatitude (*ānanda*) is the point of rest in the supreme state; creative capacity (*iśāna*) is the point of rest in the will; and the wave (*ūrmi*) is the point of rest in expansion. This wave is the principle of the power of the act.

'In this (listing) the preceding three aspects of cognition have a solar nature inasmuch as they are substantiated by the luminous part; those which follow have a lunar (or "communicated") nature, since in them predominates the serenity which is substantiated by repose. Up to this moment there is no insertion in act. When, however, act is inserted into will and rulership, whereby we speak of "willed" or "being ruled", then, at that moment, two differentiations appear: the semi-vowel RA, by virtue of the solar luminosity, and the semi-vowel LA by virtue of the point of rest, because RA and LA have, respectively, the natures of luminosity and of inertia. What is willed and ruled does not appear as a manifest external object, because if it had manifest (objective) form, then it would be a product, and not will or rulership. Therefore, because they are not manifest as objects RA and LA are regarded only as semi-vowels (they are) not precise as are the consonants. These four letters are, then, neutral since they contain the likeness of both (vowels and consonants); they are R, Ṛ, L, Ḷ.

'When there occurs the efflux of supreme power (*anuttara*) and of beatitude (*ānanda*) into the will etc., we have the two vowels E and O. Then, by another union of beatitude and supreme power, with will we have AI and AU, this is the power of the act which is symbolized by E, AI, O, AU. When the power of the act terminates its function, when all that which has been created enters into the Supreme Power (*anuttara*), it (which has been created), before this occurs, remains in the form of a point (*bindu*) symbolized by AM, as it is essentially autoconsciousness.

'There, in the point, arises the emanation of Supreme Power (*anuttara*) which is symbolized by AḤ. Therefore, it is said that these sixteen vowels constitute the seed of cognition, while the womb is represented by the consonants. From the Supreme Power arises the series of the gutturals and from pure will the series of the palatals; from objectivated will arises the series of the linguals and dentals and from expansion the series of the labials, that is to say, a set of five through conjunction with five sorts of powers. From the same threefold will arise YA, RA, LA; from expansion the letter VA, from sole threefold will ŚA, ṢA, SA: from efflux (*visarga*) the letter HA and from the conjunction of the two wombs KSHA. This is the aspect of God called Supreme Power (*anuttara*) which is represented by his being lord of the family of the powers which it contains. One of the powers which belong to his family, the power of emanation, is that from which (beginning from the aspect of beatitude and ending at objective creation) individual cognitions, symbolized by the consonants etc. (brought about in the Cosmic Consciousness after the first quivering flicker therein) are realized in the objective aspect of categories (*tattva*). And this emanation is in three modes: atomic (*āṇava*) which is the form of the point of rest in limited thought; efficient (*śākta*) which has the character of the awakening of limited thought; and *śāmbhava* which consists of the reabsorption (*pralaya*) of limited thought; therefore the emanation is the divine power capable of creating all things. When all this cognition remains indistinct then God is one. When, afterwards, this manifests itself in a twofold aspect—inasmuch as it assumes the form of either seed or womb—then, in cognition itself appear two aspects, namely, that of the possessor of power (*śaktiman*) and that of power (*śakti*).' (The *Tantrasāra* of Abhinavagupta, Bombay 1918, pp. 12–17)

There is, therefore, no necessity for the presence of

images on the surfaces of *maṇḍalas*. Instead of representations, it is enough to have the symbolical syllable, the mysterious matrix of their form. Indeed, we may say that the *mantras* are more real than such images, since those are appearances suited to our *karmic* limitations, they are figures by means of which that which has no form becomes, through artifice, accessible to us, a cloak (imagined by ourselves) under which is hidden an invisible essence although it is, so to speak, immediately perceptible in the concentration of meditation which may make us sharers of that essence. In other words, it is a relationship of reciprocity between the being which is revealed and the person to whom it is revealed. And so the latter, in a certain sense, himself moulds the aspect of the revealed being, adapting it to his own conceptions and to his *karmic* maturity. In this way, he appears as 'Man among men, God among Gods, Brahma with the Brahmas' (*Siddhi*, pp. 764–5). That same Śākyamuni who was born a man among men may appear in various guises to different beings (*sKyabs ạgro bdun bcu pa*, p. 9). Such is, indeed, the character of the imaginary body (*nirmāṇakāya*) of the Buddha. In addition to this, there exists the mystical body (*sambhogakāya*) which can be contemplated solely by Bodhisattvas of the tenth earth, led up to that plane by their own meditations. In the choir of the blessed ones who have reached that same spiritual maturity, they, in those spheres outside space, will witness the revelation of the law which is suited to their particular degree of elevation. This comes about from the second revulsion of planes (*āśrayaparāvṛtti*) by virtue of which all terrestrial forms are overcome and a transcendent aspect is assumed. Both the first and the second aspects are adapted to creatures of varying degrees of purity and are relative to them. But the supreme essence, the *dharmakāya*, the absolute plane, the substance of all things beyond all form, transcends them both, an immaculate and luminous matrix.

All this is no innovation. In the whole of India it has always been believed that man accedes to God by degrees. The Absolute in its essence transcends all human thought. *Na iti, na iti* says of it the Upanishad: 'if of him you predicate some attribute, I will reply that it is not so'. But his manifestation is adapted to creatures and it varies from the coarsest forms suited for the conversion of uncouth minds to forms which are most noble and subtle. From the adoration (*upāsana*) of idols to that concentration of soul in which the spirit is drowned in a sea of light, the way is long, but its stages are adapted to the various capacities of believers.

'Brahma whose essence is thought, individual, entire, incorporeal, comes to be imagined corporeal for the benefit of worshippers' (*Śāktānandatar*, p. 52) and, again, 'Men, in diverse manners and according to their various inclinations, see the Whole accessible through reflection (*dhyāna*)' (ibid., p. 62.) Or, as the Agnipurāṇa says: Godhead, who has no form, assumes different forms in order to help the devotees: the manifestations of the unmanifested has only an instrumental value, inasmuch as it frees consciousness from the veil of *māyā*.

In this principle it is implicit that the Gods, as images of our conscious principle, must disappear and vanish when the luminosity of consciousness, pure and without form, shines within us. Therefore, in the gnostic liturgy of India a mirror is employed. This serves to remind the mystic that the images before which the rite is performed are reflections to be burned by the fire of gnosis; they have no nature of their own, they are but creations of our karmic state. When there appear to the conscious principle of a dead man (during the state of existence intermediate between death and rebirth) images of the Gods either beatific or terrifying, the master reminds him that

'all these luminous fabrics will appear to join together in thy heart. O son of noble family, they are the contrivances of thy thought; they come from no other place (than from thy thought), have, therefore, no attachment for them and remain, without fear, in a state of mental inactivity. Then those images and lights will dissolve within thee and thou wilt become a perfect Buddha.

'In that moment thou must remember the instructions for inducing this recognition, which the Master gave thee during thy life. If thou wilt remember the meaning of them and wilt believe in those images which have appeared before thee, it will be like a meeting between mother and son, or the recognition of persons known not long ago, as when one has made a good resolution; if these images are really recognized as thy own images, if thou believest in them, since they are the immutable path of the pure, absolute plane, a durable state of ecstasis will arise in thee, and the intellect dissolving itself in the sphere of the Absolute, thou wilt become a perfect Buddha on the plane of intelligible forms, from which there is no turning back.

'O son, the terrible and frightening apparitions which thou mayest see, are also images of thy own thought; so, also, thou must recognize light as the brightness of thy own thought. By such recognition one becomes consubstantiated with the Buddhas. There is no doubt about this, and in a single instant one becomes a perfect Buddha. Therefore remember! O son of noble family, if, of thyself, thou do not so recognize, thou wilt have fear. Then the calm deities will manifest themselves in the aspect of the God of Death, the images of thy own thought will transform themselves into the demon and thou wilt wander in the heaven of transmigration. O son of noble family, if thou do not recognize that these images are of thy own thought, even if thou hast been learned in the holy scriptures and hast observed the precepts of the Law, for a whole cosmic age thou shalt not be consubstantiated with the Buddhas. But if one recognizes that these are images of one's own thought one will be instantly consubstantiated with the Buddhas. If one does not recognize that these are images of one's own thought, immediately after death, and in the state of intermediate existence (in which is revealed the plane of ideas) these will be manifested as images of the God of Death. The figure of the God of Death is as large as the expanse of the sky, in his median measurement like Sumeru, in his smallest aspect eighteen times thy own body, and it covers the universe. With his upper teeth he bites his lip. His eyes (blaze) like crystal. His hair is twisted round on the top of his head. His belly is huge and his waist slender. He holds in his hands a bludgeon and roars with a loud voice "Strike. Kill". He drinks brains, tears heads from bodies and plucks out hearts. Thus he comes covering the universe with his face. O son of noble family, when such an apparition shall manifest itself unto thee, have no fear, be not afraid. Since thy body is no more a material body, but a mental one constituted by the propensities of thy *karma*, even if he kill thee and cut thee in pieces, thou canst not die. Verily, have no fear since thy own form is void and the manifestations of the God of Death appear in the luminosity of thy own thoughts and are deprived of reality. The void can no more molest the void. These things are but the contrivance of thy thought. Outside of that nothing exists, neither calm Gods, nor terrifying Gods with diverse heads, nor deities that drink blood, nor the rainbow in which it may seem to thee that thou mergest, nor the frightful figure of the God of Death, nor any terror. Of this there is no doubt.'

What do these deities mean which we see represented in *maṇḍalas*? They are divinities in beatific or terrifying shapes, alone or coupled, they are often shown in slightly varied forms, although they may bear the same name; they are susceptible of transformation into new hypostases, of various colours, shown now with one and now with several faces, sometimes with two and at other times with many hands, deities which gnosis assures us do not exist objectively, but that are only the projections of our own thought. Why do these deities appear in such diverse forms?

They are, as we have seen, symbols by means of which consciousness fixes, so to speak, the restless turmoil of forces that succeed each other and battle in the psyche. Only by means of these symbols can the psyche focus these forces, take cognizance of them and eliminate them in a definitive process of *lusis* or deliverance, without which there can be no salvation. This means that such symbols must be taken, not as objective realities, but as provisional figurations which have been formed by a reciprocal exchange between the Absolute Consciousness and the individual consciousness and suited to the latter. When these are recognized for what they are, that is to say reflections of Being, they are dissolved by degrees, into the original, motionless luminosity. They indicate the various stages of Return, but in order that they may play their proper part in this process which produces palingenesis, they must be interpreted. The different colours of the faces, the variable number of hands, the implements grasped, are so many translations into visible signs of the truth which the mystic must relive in the spiritual drama which, surging up from the depths of his soul, regenerates him.

These truths, owing to such a technique, live no more as remote and chilly certainties, lifeless, theological theorems, but are transfigured into psychological forces which act from within and transform the whole being of the mystic from its very depths. Let us take as examples two images, those of Heruka and Vajrabhairava which are the most popular deities of Buddhist esoterism, and let us see then how the initiatory Schools 'read' them.

Śrī Cakra-Saṃvara (Heruka) is thus described:[1]

In the middle of the lotus, on the solar seat, is the God of

[1] This description and symbology have been drawn and summarized from various sources.

the deep blue body. He has four faces. The first (in the middle) is of deep blue, that to the left green, that at the back of his head red, and that to the right yellow. Each face has three eyes. He has twelve hands. On his forehead he wears a diadem of five-pointed *vajras*. With his outstretched right leg he crushes the head of Kālabhairava who has four arms; two are joined together in the attitude of adoration, in the second on the right he has the magic drum (*ḍamaru*) and in the second on the left he has the sword. The left leg is drawn back and tramples on the chest of Red Kali who also has four arms; two are joined together in the attitude of adoration and of the other two that on the right holds a skull (*kapāla*) and that on the left a *khatvaṅga*.[1]

'(Heruka) with his two pincipal arms embraces Vajravārahī, while, at the same time, holding in his right hand a five-pointed *vajra* and in his left the small bell (to symbolize that he is the union of illumination and compassion). The hands of the two arms underneath are in the attitude of menace (*tarjanīmudrā*); with them he holds and stretches out at the level of his eyes a vestment made of the white and blood-stained skin of an elephant and with the left hand the left foot of this skin. In his other right hands he holds aloft, respectively, the magic drum, the hatchet, the knife and the trident. In his left hands the *khatvaṅga* (marked with the *vajra* symbol of illumination), a cranium full of blood (symbol of supreme beatitude), the adamantine noose and the head of Brahma with four faces. He bears the ascetic forelock marked with a double *vajra* arranged as a cross (*viśvavajra*). On each head is a diadem of black *vajras* on which are fixed five skulls above and five below. On the left side of his face he has a slightly sloping crescent. The faces are deformed and made terrifying by the four jutting teeth

[1] A *khatvaṅga* is an implement used by ascetics; it is a sort of club on which are fixed a freshly severed head, another in a state of putrefaction and a skull.

and the sneering grimace. He has nine modes: three of the body, robust, heroic and ugly; three of words, savage, terrible and awe-inspiring; three of the spirit, compassionate, dignified and serene. At his belt he wears an apron of tiger-skins. Suspended from his neck is a garland of fifty freshly severed human heads strung on a thread of human guts. He is marked with six seals (*mudrā*) and his body is smeared with the ashes of burnt corpses. The coupling of the "mother" and "father"[1] signifies the fusion of the two coefficients of salvation, that is, on the one hand, the "means", namely compassion or the active element (since this "means" when it has attained particular efficacy permeates the most vital parts of the body), and, on the other hand, "wisdom". During the union with the "mother", the "moon", that is the thought of illumination seated in the head, melts and permeates the whole body. From it proceeds the "great bliss of the mean" which symbolizes meditation on the four fundamentals of liberation which have as their object the insubstantiality of the All, identified with mystical wisdom: this bliss is symbolized by the *khatvaṅga*, the skull symbolizing that he is beyond all notions of substance and no substance.

'Each has a crown of five skulls, to signify the possession of the five gnoses. All this suggests purification from thirst for action etc., liberation from mental obscuration, evocation of all the Buddhas, the excision of false concepts concerning the extreme theses and the errors of the three "doors" (that is body, word and spirit), the piercing of all moral infections and the union with pure consciousness, the submission of the two extreme theses, namely that of eternity or of the continual existence of *saṃsāra*, and that of annihilation, namely the non-existence (of the individual) in *nirvāṇa*. In a word, the submission of the whole phenomenal world by means of the concept of insubstantiality.

'The elephant skin is the symbol of ignorance, the drum

[1] For these images are shown as coupled. *Yab yum* in Tibetan.

that of the good news of the Law, the axe because it cuts out *saṃsāra* and its roots. He clutches a knife because he slashes pride and sins. He holds a trident because he puts an end to greed, wrath and mental perturbation. The skull is filled with blood because he is beyond material and non-material things. He holds the adamantine noose because gnosis reveals the essence of creatures. He holds, by the hair, the head of Brahma to indicate that he is free of all illusions.

'The skulls that form the necklace of the God signify the incorporation of light that proceeds from the peace attained by the suppression of all extremes. The twelve hands indicate purification from all spot or stain as regards the interpretation of the twelve-fold causal concatenation. The deformed faces signify the denial of all theories, the sneer of the projecting teeth indicates the overcoming of the four Māra (see p. 86). The upstanding ascetic's tuft symbolizes the conception of ascending merit, the garland of *vajras*, quiescence in the quintuple gnosis which is attained when merit reaches its greatest development. The God has three eyes because with his wisdom he discovers everything in all three times and in the triple space. He bears on the top of his head a double *vajra* in the form of a cross because, with four-fold action, he accomplishes the good of all creatures. The six seals signify the perfection of the methods (literally "paths") which lead to the six mystical perfections. He is adorned with all the magnificence of that spiritual serenity which is the conglomeration of the five Buddhas and of the four mothers.

'In front of the Blessed One is the head of Vajravārahī, whose body is red because dedicated to the good of creatures. She has only one face to indicate the essential sameness of all things, two hands, because truth is twofold, absolute and relative, and three eyes. She is naked with dishevelled hair because she has been set free from the illusions that hide the essence of things. She wears a girdle adorned with portions of skulls because she bestows supreme bliss and with her right hand, in the gesture of menace (*tarjanīmudrā*), she clutches the *vajra* and terrifies the demons of the ten points of space.

'Since she is the symbol of intuition of the universe's insubstantiality, she is like the fire which at the end of the ages destroys the worlds. She is resplendent with solar brilliance as she expresses the possession of the purest wisdom. She rejoices in blood, she drips blood, she presses with her legs the thighs of the "father", consubstantial with the Great Compassion, since she accomplishes the good of creatures while remaining in the highest beatitude which consists in the Supreme Vision. She is decked with five seals, but is not smeared with ashes, she wears a garland of fifty skulls and has upon her forehead a diadem of five skulls.'

And, now, here is a description of Vajrabhairava:

'Mahāvajrabhairava must have a body of very deep-blue colour, nine faces, thirty-four arms and sixteen feet. The legs on the left side are advanced and those on the right drawn back. He is able to swallow the three worlds. He sneers and roars. His tongue is arched. He gnashes his teeth and his eyebrows are wrinkled. His eyes and his eyebrows flame like the cosmic fire at the time of the destruction of the universe. His hair is yellow and stands on end. He menaces the Gods of the material and the non-material spheres. He frightens even the terrifying deities. He roars out the word *p'ain* with a voice like the rumble of thunder. He devours flesh, marrow and human fat and drinks blood. He is crowned with five awe-inspiring skulls and is adorned with a garland made of fifteen freshly severed heads. His sacrificial cord is a black serpent. The ornaments in his ears etc. are of human bones. His belly is huge, his body naked and his penis erect. His eyebrows, eyelids, beard and body-hair flame like the cosmic fire at the end of the ages. His middle face is that of a buffalo. It is horned and expresses violent anger. Above it, and between the horns, projects a yellow face.

'The erect ascetic's tuft signifies that he is consubstantial with the five mystical gnoses. His aspect is terrifying because he repels adverse forces (*Māra*). His sixteen feet are symbols of the sixteen species of insubstantiality. His nakedness means that all things are without birth. The erect penis means that he is consubstantial with the Supreme Beatitude. His thirty-four arms are symbols of the thirty-four coefficients of Illumination: the knife because he kills ignorance; the hatchet because he tests false imaginings regarding subject and object; the pestle to signify the concentration of cognition; the razor because he cuts away sin; the goad to indicate the submission of the body and the word; the axe because he hacks away error from the mind; the lance becauses he annihilates false theories; the arrow because he transfixes erroneous imaginings; the hook because he pulls (along to salvation); the club because he rips down the veil which is caused by *karma*; the *khatvaṅga* because his nature is consubstantial with the thought of Illumination; the disk because he puts in motion the Wheel of the Law; the *vajra* because he is consubstantial with the fifth gnosis; the hammer because he smashes avarice; the sword because he grants various magic powers such as those of the sword etc.; the drum because with the Supreme Beatitude which this symbolizes, he harmonizes all the Tathāgatas; the skull filled with blood because he incites to the observance of the vow; the head of Brahmā because, in his pity, he accomplishes the good of all creatures; the shield because he triumphs over all the works of Māra; the foot because he grants to the meditator the same rank as the Buddhas; the noose because he possesses (literally "ties") the highest wisdom; the bow because he triumphs over the three worlds; the guts because he explains the insubstantiality of things;

the bell which indicates consubstantiality with the supreme gnosis; the hand because he is able to do all things; the rags gathered in cemeteries because he destroys the veil of ignorance which causes us to think that things have their own essence; the man impaled upon a stake because he fully understands the concept that all things are deprived of substance; the little stove (of triangular shape) to symbolize the germinal light (*'od gsal*); the freshly severed head because he is full of that ambrosia which is compassion; the hand in the gesture of menace because he terrifies the demons; the three-pointed lance as a symbol of the concept that spirit, word and body have a single essence; a fluttering piece of stuff because all things are as *māyā*. The beings upon which he tramples serve to symbolize the mystical powers which come from him.'

These personages of the Diamond Vehicle which we have described serve to demonstrate how inexhaustibly rich is the Buddhist Pantheon. When the masters sink into their meditations, from the depths of their psyche there emerge revelations (on which they concentrate their minds as the provisional support of successive ineffable ecstasies) which assume forms and aspects often different from those we have already noted. At the moment he prepares himself for the evocation, the meditator starts from the conviction that certain truths will appear in certain forms. Their number and their aspect have been fixed by the long habit of former experiences.

The number must not be changed and was strictly defined in the *maṇḍala* schemes which almost always reproduce pictorially, for the rest, the paradigms of the doctrinal teaching. The number could, indeed, not be altered without shaking the foundations of all Buddhist theological structure. Nevertheless, when these forces had to be visualized and represented in the form of deities, the meditator could not escape from the mysterious impulses of his own subconsciousness. During his absorption in meditation, there could break through and take shape in these images, from the depths of his psyche, recollections which had been temporarily lulled, traces of which he was no longer aware and left by encounters that went unheeded, unforeseen digressions, instincts which had been repressed. This, indeed, does happen and it explains the great number of methods for realization of the particular truths into which the different Tantras plunge deeply. There is hardly any great Master who has not composed *sādhanas* (here: ways or methods how to visualize a deity); who has not, that is, recorded in writing, the visions which appeared to his spirit during the time of spiritual concentration. From the mere fact that these had appeared to him, that they materialized, he rightly considered them to be real. They had assumed forms, they were no longer jostled about, obscure, in the depths of his subconscious; a new possibility of incorporation of the subconscious had taken shape and it was necessary to make a careful note of it, since in others these same visions might be repeated.

What happened in Buddhism occurred also in the Hinduist Schools, which have always regarded images as symbols that only the initiated can read.

The *Śakti*, to take an example, may be represented—among many other ways—with four arms. In the lower left arm she holds a bow with a string of bees, in the lower right arm five arrows of various different flowers, in the upper left arm the red noose, and in the upper right arm the hook. These symbols can be understood in three different ways—the vulgar or coarse, the subtle and the extremely subtle. In the first way, they are regarded as they appear to the eye—that is with no understanding of their more secret sense. In the second way they translate the *mantra* into visible terms. The bow corresponds to the syllable THAṂ, the noose to the syllable HŪṂ and so forth. In the third way, the bow is the mind, the five arrows are the five subtle elements—that is matter in its quintuple quintessential form—the noose represents the passions, the hook, anger.

But if the *maṇḍala* is a guide to salvation, inasmuch as it arouses liberating cognition, it follows that the *maṇḍala* must assume an infinite number of aspects. In Buddhism the immense spiritual or intellectual variety of creatures has been recognized from the beginning, so that truth, in order to be operative and penetrate into men's hearts, must be refracted in a thousand modes. An absolute, dogmatic, inalterable truth would be useless. The Buddha behaves with regard to creatures as a physician towards his patients. A physician knows that sickness, taken by itself, is an abstraction. Only, within the framework, so to speak, of a malady there are sick men. Thus, also, in the world of *māyā* there are persons, each one differing from the other by the imprint of *karma* and by the propensities it causes. The truth that is salvation for one man, is perdition to another, just as the formulae of the snake-charmer, if wrongly employed, kill him who uses them. Hence, the Buddha, who is rightly called the Supreme Physician, knows how to distribute truth by adapting it to his disciples and to those who harken to him. That quality in the Buddha which is the most honoured by the theologians is the ability to know what are the appropriate means to be adopted (*upāyakauśalyatā*). So, in all Indian gnostic tradition great importance is attached to the *guru*, the master, to him who must produce the revulsion of the adept. Lore, by itself, is of no use unless it be wisely employed through a direct relationship between teacher and pupil. They must become spiritually attuned. There must be not merely a cold, intellectual relationship as between master and scholar, but a current of life; not a general transmission of vague ideas and concepts, but an intimate, vital contact which, like blood, renews the spirit of the neophyte. It is a relationship which the mystics define as resembling that between a cow and her calf.

The *guru*, in his wisdom, brings to light, gradually, that which was hidden in our depths, and, little by little, we perceive that the horizon around us becomes more clear. Thus, we are entirely involved in this work of clarification which illuminates us and, at the same time, gives form and shape to those projections of our spirit which correspond to that degree of maturity by which, from time to time, truth reveals itself to us, in one aspect or another, but always more lofty and complete according to our own spiritual intensity. Ours is not an inert receptivity but a creative concomitance by which truth while illuminating us is, as it were, our daughter.

This complicated revaluation of the individual, this adaptation of truth to him, this correspondence between the manifestation of God and the spiritual intensity of Man, has led, of didactic necessity, to a scholastic division of creatures into different fundamental types. According as we belong to one type or to another, one mode of teaching rather than another will be recommended, although the *guru*, within these limits, may move about as he will, from time to time, in his perspicacity, addressing himself to the outstanding qualities in the inevitable spiritual 'polyvalence' of the neophyte.

On this principle of the diversity of creatures (and therefore of the symbols which may be the most suited to conduct them along the path of salvation) is based the quadruple division of the esoteric Scriptures known as Tantras. These are the expression of a spiritual attitude which has found its most complete definition in gnosis. Gnosis, which assumes many aspects and is common to many countries, translates in analogous symbols the same spiritual anxiety and affirms, often in almost the same words, the identity of the human and divine natures. Gnosis implies an initiatory baptism, a liberating knowledge, it rehabilitates most ancient religious intuitions, but it interprets them, nevertheless, in new ways, as allegories of the drama within us through which palingenesis is accomplished. Gnosis flourished at one and the same time from one end to the other of the ancient world. Pao-p'u Tzu in China developed the alchemic aspect of gnosis, conceiving, according to Taoist tradition, the corporeal immortality of the adept. The aim of all the Tantras is to teach the ways whereby we may set free the divine light which is mysteriously present and shining in each one of us, although it is enveloped in an insidious web of the psyche's weaving. Mani, Valentinus, Bardesanes and the author of the *Pistis Sophia* were moved by similar aspirations and they form so many bridges linking the ideas of oriental esoterism with Hellenistic gnosis.

The Tantras, in which Indian gnosis is expressed, were, for the most part, written and disseminated in lands on India's confines where, along the caravan-routes, meetings and exchanges of ideas were much facilitated. The Tantras, as I have said, came to be divided into four groups called, respectively, *Kriyā*, *Caryā*, *Yoga* and *Anuttara*. These groups recognize the diversity of men as ineradicable and, consequently, they describe a number of psychological categories. With these categories as a foundation they prescribe, in detail and for each man, a particular liturgy. Truth is revealed in the way best suited to him and this, not only with the aim of carrying him along to salvation, but also of conferring upon him some magical power.

All human—and also divine—beings are included in these divisions. According to Buddhism, the Gods, too, who are assigned to the various paradises, are born and die. The divine condition is not a definitive one but a plane with which, by the process of meditation, the mystic can consubstantiate himself by raising himself spiritually to such a height and by participating in a timeless Presence, in its glory.

The matter of the world is made up of passion and even the Gods who dwell in the lowest of the three spheres of existence, the *Kāmaloka*, cannot escape from it. This passion is revealed in some particular manner, by a smile, a glance, a pressure of the hand, sexual connection—four ways of expressing passion which correspond to the four classes of Gods which were defined already in the dogmatics of ancient times.

With regard to men, it is well known that some are inclined to ritual as a means of overcoming the stains of sin, provided that, of course, the rite is properly conceived as a symbol of spiritual purification. For such people (whom the Buddhist masters identify with the Brahmins, the sacerdotal caste obedient to the letter but very often unaware of, or little concerned with, the spirit which should animate ceremonies) there is provided a special class of Tantras, that of the *Kriyātantras*, particularly devoted to liturgical complications. It is a homoeopathic treatment by which it is sought, gradually, to open the eyes of the officiant and to show him what a complex instrument of psychological revulsion he has at his disposal, provided that he knows how to understand its meaning. The gesture (*mudrā*) of the Gods is here a smile.

The *Caryātantras* are suited for the *rje rigs*, the nobleman, in whom a respect for ceremonial is accompanied by a capacity for spiritual meditation. These Tantras are addressed to persons who may experience the dawn of spiritual anxiety and in whom there may be present the intellectual and spiritual prerequisites for the Return. The gesture here is a look. The *Yogatantras* are addressed to the *rgyal rigs*, of royal family, powerful men, who cannot manage to renounce the goods of this world. For their meditation is offered the *maṇḍala* with a lavish display of Gods, Goddesses and acolytes which are shown in this illustrated diagram like the court of a king in his palace. For one must begin by speaking to such men a language which they can understand, if one does not wish to drive them away for ever. What would be the use of renunciation and sacrifice to those who love the joy of living, if they are, to begin with, ignorant of the fact that real beatitude is an overcoming of that which they most desire? The gesture here is an embrace.

The *Anuttaratantras* are reserved for the creatures who sin most, who do not distinguish good from evil, who lead impure lives. It is on the very fault itself by which they are sullied that is built up slowly the work of redemption. The gesture here is union.

Other reasons are also given for this division; it may be founded on certain predispositions which exist in individuals. In some it is mental confusion that predominates. They are slow and dull, their intelligence is not luminous. For these the *Kriyātantras* are suited. In other men such darkness is not marked, and their intelligence is lively. For these the *Caryātantras* are suitable. For those in whom passion and irascibility are present to a middling and a slight degree, the *Yogatantras* are suited. When, however, the three defects exist in the highest degree, the *Anuttaratantras* are to be recommended.

Hence, as the ritual is adapted to individual adepts, the *maṇḍalas* are very great in number. In some of the Tantras of the *Yogatantra* class they can be counted in hundreds.

Of course, the basic repartition of the *maṇḍalas* is founded on the divisions between creatures which we have already indicated.

The first type of classification was obviously suggested by the division of creatures into five mystical families (*kula*, *rigs*), in which is accomplished a differentiation of the reality that is potential in the Absolute and which on the mystical plane is represented by the supreme pentad. There is obtained thus a quintuple typology, that is to say a family of the Tathāgatas (Vairocana), one of the *Vajra* or Diamond (Akṣobhya), one of the Jewel (Ratnasaṃbhava), one of the Lotus (Amitābha) and one of Operative Activity (Amoghasiddhi). The neophyte must, first of all, find out, with the help of his master, which is the particular family to which he belongs, and then choose the *maṇḍala* which corresponds to that family. Generally speaking, each family has its own special *maṇḍala*. However, some Schools admit that it may be possible to represent symbolically the five families in one synthetic *maṇḍala* where these are all included and summarized.

At other times, the choice of the *maṇḍala* is determined by that mystical plane with which the devotee may wish to attune himself, that is to say with one of the three or four essential aspects of reality, beyond phenomenal appearances—the physical (*kāya*, *sku*), the verbal (*vāc*, *gsuṅ's*) and the mental (*manas*, *t'ugs*) to which many Schools add that of activity (*karma*, *p'rin las*).

Again, the choice of *maṇḍala* may be suggested by the intrinsic qualities of the persons who are to be guided by it (as soon as they know how to read in it its mystical meaning) to the revelation of Supreme Truth which is symbolically represented in its diagrams and figures. There are some people who do not manage to understand the meaning of a doctrine unless it is explained to them in all its details. There are also those who understand immediately and to whom it is sufficient to give a brief explanation, since they grasp it all at once. Finally there is a third category of men that comes in between the two foregoing. It is made up of people who are not so quick to comprehend by a few indications, but who, also, are not so slow-witted as to need everything to be explained in the smallest detail. These distinctions between different sorts of possible disciples, or rather of persons whom the Master may be able to guide towards the right comprehension of the truth, is found, indeed, in the dogmatical works. For the first category there is the detailed *maṇḍala*, for the third the abbreviated or succinct *maṇḍala* and for the category in between there is the intermediate *maṇḍala*.

Then, some men have inclinations which so predominate that (as I have said above) there can be no question of extirpating them suddenly, they must—as the psychoanalysts now say—be 'transferred' to another plane and applied to other uses.

In some persons passion (*rāga, ḥdod c'ags*) is ardent; in others it is wrath (*krodha, k'ro ba*); in others, again, it is mental confusion (*moha, gti mug*); while in some it is avarice (*mātsarya, ser sna*) that predominates. A particular sort of *maṇḍala* is indicated for each of these four types of people, one which is appropriate to the moral propensities which seem to predominate in the disciple. Furthermore, the special devotion which some may have for certain divinities is not overlooked. It is of little importance if these do not figure in the Buddhist pantheon, and therefore do not have the same value for salvation as a real Buddhist symbol. In the Tantras there is no objection to accepting the divinities of the profane (*hjig rten pa*) whether they be the eight Mahādevas, Viṣṇu, Rudra or even the planets and the constellations. The important thing is that there should be faith. This is the sentiment that must be worked on and whose presence in the soul of the neophytes is a necessary and indispensable prerequisite if they are to rise slowly and by degrees to supreme Salvation. Such cults may constitute inferior forms of religious experience but they indicate, all the same, a spiritual sensibility which is but awaiting education and refinement. In short, they form the first rung of a tall ladder, the initial phase of a progressive purification and sublimation. It is, therefore, no wonder if, in designing the *maṇḍalas*, account is taken also of the spiritual capacity of some persons to be led on the good way by their own devotion to certain divine manifestations even if these do not seem, at first glance, to be orthodox. This is so deep-rooted and vital a principle of Buddhism that some followers of the Shingon sect have attempted to incorporate even Christian symbols into their *maṇḍalas*.

Every shape and form that arises in the soul, every link which, in a mysterious way, joins us to the Universal Life and unites us, maybe without our being aware of it, to Man's most ancient experience, the voices which reach us from the depths of the abyss, all are welcomed with almost affectionate solicitude. Buddhism does not desire that such life of the soul should be scattered. It is of no importance if these images, visions, fears and hopes are not entirely suited to our own vision. They are a legacy which Man carries with him from his birth. They have a positive, real existence like the things we see and feel. They are an irrepressible element of our persons. If, with the rule of reason, we should desire to thrust them back down into the depths of our souls, they would burst forth, all the same, sudden and destructive. It is better, then, to assume possession of them at the first and then by degrees to transfigure them, just as one passes from the outer enclosure of the *maṇḍala*, successively, through the others until one reaches the central point, the primordial equipoise regained after the experience of life.

All this, in any case, demands that the Master should display much good judgement before teaching the disciple. It is the former's task to study the pupil's character, to make sure that the chosen way will turn out beneficial and not harmful for him. There is the classical example of the celebrated Tibetan poet and mystic Milaraspa, a pupil of Marpa; he had demanded with insistence to be initiated into the mysteries of Buddhist esoterism and, in desperation, he had betaken himself to the Master Marpa, his soul riotous with passion and hatred. Milaraspa, after his father's death, had seen his relations turn against him. They had reduced him to misery, seized everything and caused his mother to die of starvation. They had forced him to live the life of a wandering beggar. For many years a thirst for vengeance tormented him. Then he devoted himself to the study of Black Magic and by means of spells he procured the death of his enemies. But still he found no peace for his spirit. He came to Marpa's dwelling in search of the serenity which would render him completely indifferent to the disappointments and sorrows of life, in the certainty that everything is ephemeral and futile. He wanted to extinguish the fire that burned within him for his spirit was untamed and passion was always ready to burst forth violently. Marpa understood his disciple's ills and received him into his own School where he was set to perform hard tasks so that the rebellious spirit might be bent. Marpa humiliated him, struck him, ordered him to build a house of many storeys and various times made him pull it down. However, little by little, under this harsh discipline, Milaraspa was subdued. Passion died down and his heart opened to the serene beatitude of ecstasis. Henceforth he was for ever calmed, he was no longer the slave of his own psyche, but its lord.

But how can the Master be sure of having divined the character of the disciple? Does he not dispose of some means by which he can verify whether his diagnosis be right, if the disciple who comes to him can really be healed by the way the Master suggests? Or, to express ourselves in Tantric terminology, does the disciple really belong to the particular 'family' where the psychological process which corresponds to that family can be safely applied to him? How can it be verified whether his 'family' really is such a one and that the Master has not made a mistake?

Generally speaking, the method is twofold, that of the casting of the flower and that of the dream. We shall discuss them shortly.

4

THE LITURGY OF THE MAṆḌALA

THE liturgy which accompanies the construction and design of a *maṇḍala* is very complex. First of all, this act presupposes, normally, the presence of a Master who performs the ceremonies and that of one or more disciples who have asked to be initiated into the mysteries revealed, in symbolical form, by the *maṇḍala*. Access to the *maṇḍala* is, in fact, the culmination of a long and patient apprenticeship and a proof of the spiritual maturity which the Master has recognized in the neophytes. Scholastic and doctrinal preparation has, little by little, eliminated ignorance which clouds the intellect and those errors and perplexities which are characteristic of earthly experience. Then, baptism is sought so that the congenital stains which inevitably are associated with our human limitations may be wiped out. It is a sacrament which enables us to make real in ourselves the revulsion from this to the other plane and which facilitates, by provoking a psychological drama that revolutionizes our interior life, the Return, the palingenesis.

The first thing that must be done is to purify the officiant. No one can engage in the rite if he is not spiritually and also physically pure. Fasting and bathing are prescribed by the rules.

Great care must be taken in choosing the place and the time. A propitious day must be selected and a place near a river's bank or the seashore, to the north of a town, or the proper chapel in a temple, and it should be secluded. Then, the ground on which the *maṇḍala* is to be drawn must be cleared of all stones, charcoal or animal remains. The ground must be flat and smooth so that it may from the very first indicate, by its appearance, its similarity to the transcendent plane, the adamantine plane into which the *maṇḍala* will be transfigured by the rites. Then the demons must be driven away, that is to say Māra and his acolytes. Māra is the God of Death, but he is also the God of Love, the symbol of all that makes us the slaves of lapse and attachment to life. He is quadruple, *skandha, kleśa, mṛtyu* and *devaputramāra, pravṛtti,* that is to say the five constituents of the human personality (which have been mentioned above), the infections, or all the thoughts that hide the light of truth; death, and finally Māra as God personified, the symbol of those three which are the companions of our life and also the inevitable heralds of death.

The elimination of Māra—that coincides with the purification of the site—is accomplished by the evocation of the Goddess Earth of her who Śākyamuni, after the Night of Bodhgaya when his Awakening took place, invoked to witness the Illumination which had been achieved. Then the earth is touched with the *vajra*, the indispensable instrument in Great Vehicle liturgy, and thus is transformed into *vajra*; becomes diamond.

The symbolism of the ritual act is clear. A *maṇḍala*, as I have said above, is an ideal Bodhgaya, an 'adamantine plane', that is an incorruptible surface, the representation of the very instant in which is accomplished the revulsion to the other plane, in which one becomes Buddha. This is an experience which did not occur only once, on that famous night, and in the spirit of the Tathāgata, but which is renewed in him who, through the verbal manifestation of the Absolute represented by the 'Word of the Buddha', may realize that liberation of the consciousness which lies hidden in his depths, wrapped round with the tentacles of the psyche.

Then, as soon as the officiant and the surface have been purified, comes the actual drawing of the *maṇḍala* by means of two cords. The first is white and serves to trace the outside limits. The other is composed of five intertwined threads, each of a different colour. This is called 'the cord of gnosis' since it is employed to draw the figures of the Gods who, as has been mentioned several times, are gathered together in five main groups, to each one of which there corresponds a particular gnosis.

The fundamental divisions of the inner surface of the *maṇḍala* are drawn by following two main lines (*brahmasūtra*) from north to south and from east to west. The *brahmasūtra*, 'Thread of Brahmā', is the symbol of Meru, the *axis mundi*, to which, by homology and in the human microcosm, the median canal corresponds. This is projected on to the flat surface of the *maṇḍala* by the magical equivalence of the two directions, horizontal and vertical; it is, in the centre of the *maṇḍala*, the representation both of the axis and of the supreme point, the *brahmarandhra*, the orifice of Brahmā on the top of the skull of an individual and the limit of existence (*bhūtakoṭi*) beyond which is the other plane. Thus, in the centre of the world this is the axis around which everything revolves and develops; it indicates time and delineates space.

When the site and the arrangement of the *maṇḍala* (as *ādhāra*, *brten*—support or 'recipient') itself have been laid out, it is necessary to proceed to the invocation of the Gods who must here take up their places. They are the five 'fundamental' Gods, either alone, or each with his proper counterpart and the acolytes, according to the particular cycle which may be suggested by the officiant's inspiration. To this effect, there is placed, on each of the five basic points and on the intermediary ones, a vase filled with precious or perfumed substances and adorned with strips of cloth, flowers and sprigs of trees. Into these must be effected (through the agency of the officiant whom it will be suitable to call by the very expressive Sanskrit word *sādhaka*—'he who causes experiences to be realized') the 'descent' (*āvahana*) or 'installation' of the divine spirit that is invoked. The vases may be as many as the number of the deities represented on the surface of the *maṇḍala*. But there are exceptions and the vase may also be dispensed with.

Before the *maṇḍala* is revealed to the disciple his *adhiṣṭhāna* should be accomplished. This *adhiṣṭhāna* is like a 'state of grace', or of purity one might say, in which the neophyte will find himself when he has performed the prescribed quintuple spiritual purification.

(A) Disinterestedness: he who is preparing himself for the rite, and who, therefore, is desirous of communicating with a higher plane, must not be moved by any desire of reward, he must not have in view any gain to be obtained on this earth as a prize for the meritorious acts thus accomplished, neither must he hope for the bliss of paradise or to be caught up into those celestial choirs to which he who has cleansed himself of the stain of sin may rise. The man who would act in such an interested fashion would obscure the sacral purity. The officiant must have one intention only, that of reintegrating himself as Buddha—the reconstitution of the Threefold Diamond.

From the most ancient times the Indians, in their speculations, have recognized three fundamental aspects in Man —body, word and spirit. Although Buddhism put forward a new, and more complex dichotomy of the human personality (we may remember the theories of the five *dhātu*, of the five *skandha*, etc.), it could not disregard the basic classification. Man is the product of three planes bound together absolutely: a physical, a verbal and a spiritual. This is a dogma to which the Diamond Vehicle returns with marked satisfaction though with this innovation, namely, that the threefold plane of which the individual being is composed is imagined as having its correspondence on the transcendent plane, that is on the adamantine plane. Beneath the body, the word and the spirit, ephemeral and transitory phenomena, lies their unchangeable prototype in the identity of the *dharmakāya*, the dharma-body of the Absolute. It is this participation with the Threefold Diamond that makes up the essential nature of Gods and persons. Only such co-participation, awakened by cognition, can renew its divine essence in a creature. Therefore, during the ceremonies, whether those of initiation or of the consecration of sacred objects, when, that is to say, it is desired to introduce this essence into the person of the officiant or into the object to be consecrated, it is necessary to transpose the threefold divine plane into the one or the other.

When, for instance, the initiate prepares himself to perform the complex liturgy—prescribed by the *Guhysamāja*—so that cognition of this essential adamantine nature may be aroused in him, he recites this formula: 'OṂ, I am made of the adamantine essence of the body of all the Tathāgatas; I am made of the adamantine essence of the word of all the Tathāgatas; I am made of the adamantine essence of the spirit of all the Tathāgatas.' While this formula is being pronounced, three syllables OṂ, AḤ, HŪṂ are placed respectively on the head, the throat and the heart. That is to say the hand is placed on one of these three parts of the body at the same time as the corresponding syllable is pronounced. The three syllables are the three Diamond Seeds which introduce the divine essence into the officiant or into the object. At this moment a transfiguration takes place, that is to say, a change of personality, which is the essential motive of all Indian liturgies that conform to the ancient belief according to which, for instance, there occurs at the moment of death the transference of a father's personality into that of his son so that into the latter is carried over the secret vitality of the former, so that the father may continue to live again in the son. 'The son draws near and from above touches all the organs of the father with his own finger. Then the father transmits his own organs to the son. . . . May I deposit in thee my breath, etc. . . .' (*Kauṣītaki-Up.* Chapter II, p. 15)

(B) Taking refuge in the Trinity, that is the Buddha, the Law and the Community, the Three Masters in whose invisible but omnipresent protection he confides.

(C) Formulation of the vow to attain Supreme Illumination, that is to become Buddha, promising to tread, without hesitation or regret, the Way of the Bodhisattva. Therefore, he must not sully himself by abjuring or violating his vow, for should this come about, all merit would vanish in a trice.

(D) But what is the way that, better than any other, would make easy for the disciple a return from the troubled sea of his psyche to the calm peace of the primordial Unity? Let us call to mind what has been said above concerning the quintuple division of creatures that is symbolized in the pentad. The disciple, blindfold, is led to the eastern gate[1] of the *maṇḍala* and there receives from the Master a short stick of wood (such as is used in India for cleaning the teeth) or a flower which he must throw on to the *maṇḍala*. The section on to which these fall (which is protected by one of the five Buddhas—or their symbols) will indicate the way that is suited to the disciple.

(E) In this manner is arranged the surface on which the initiatory ceremony is to be performed. The neophyte has been admitted, though still blindfold, to the presence of the Master. However, before passing to the second part of the rite, to the real liturgical drama properly speaking, which is the access to the *maṇḍala* and, symbolically, that to the other plane, it is necessary to have warnings and premonitions

[1] East in ritual is the side facing the performer of the rite.

which will ensure that the ceremony to be performed will be successful, or else which will discourage it when conditions, or the time, or the karmic relations between the *sādhaka* and the plane which he desires to put himself into contact, are not propitious.

This direct relation between the neophyte and the spiritual plane to which he wants to ascend is fundamental. In Tibetan it is called *rten ḥbrel*, '*karma* connection', and it must be as intimate as that which binds disciple to Master, the expression of the profound syntony which should put two kindred forces into mutual agreement. If this *rten ḥbrel* is lacking any attempt would be vain. Any accord or contact would prove to be useless between the two planes which would inevitably remain alien and cut off from one another. Therefore the assurance that *rten ḥbrel* exists is a fundamental prerequisite of the liturgical act.

For such warnings the *sādhaka* relies upon dreams which play a very great part in Tantric esoterism since they encourage or dissuade from the performance of any sort of ritual act.

At nightfall the postulant must lie down and assume the position of the Buddha at the moment of Supreme *Nirvāṇa*, that is to say, stretched out at full length on his right side and with his head cupped in the palm of his hand. This is the position known as that 'of the lion'. The Master is careful to teach the neophyte some *mantras* on which he will concentrate his mind, repeating them according to the precepts, until sleep overcomes him. At dawn, when the prescribed offering has been made, he must repeat to the Master the dream which he has experienced and the Master will determine whether this is of more or of less favourable augury and will, accordingly, advise that the rite be undertaken or deferred. It is auspicious to have dreamed of the image of the Buddha, but it is inauspicious, for example, to have dreamed of a fall.

Of course, all this takes place with great attention to details, so that, by ardently concentrating his mind and being perfectly conscious of the solemnity of the occasion, the neophyte may live quite absorbed in the expectation of the mystery and may be, thus, psychologically disposed to elaborate within himself the complicated suggestions which the liturgical drama—in which he is a participant—may cause to arouse in his soul.

Perhaps I may be allowed, in this connection, to relate one of my own experiences. In 1939, when, in the Saskya monastery, I wanted to be admitted to the complicated initiation of Kyai rdo rje (Hevajra), the patron deity of the Saskya pa sect, there were undertaken during the first day the propitiatory rites of a long ceremony which started early in the morning and lasted for most of the day. The Grand Lama of Saskya gave me a leaf which had been blessed and told me to put it under my pillow and not to forget the dreams which I might possibly have during the night. I can remember that, in my dreams, I saw images of mountains and very lofty glaciers—such as I often did dream of in that country, either from the memory of the peaks I had admired or because of natural anxiety about further travel over very difficult roads. In any case, I told the abbot about the things I had seen in my dream and he could perceive in them no inauspicious sign, in fact, he interpreted the vision of mountains as of good augury and cheerfully guided me through the other phases of the ceremony.

Generally speaking, the same care not to mistake the right deity and to choose the one who may be in spiritual attunement with the neophyte, is noticeable also in the Hinduist sects, whether Śaiva or sākta, which are always very punctilious about assigning this or that *mantra* to the disciple, that is about putting him into relation with one, rather than another, spiritual plane.

With the exception of some deities which are *siddha-*

mantra, that is to say, with whom anyone can put himself into contact in all circumstances, it is necessary to be very certain of the relationship in which we stand. Hinduism has dissipated this doubt in various ways; for instance with the *kula-akula cakra*, 'the wheel of sympathy or antipathy', or else with the *raśi-cakra* 'the wheel of zodiacal signs', or again with the *nakṣatracakra* 'the wheel of the lunar mansions', and other similar means.

The first of the above-mentioned systems consists in writing a diagram in which, under five vowels that correspond to the five elements, air, fire, earth, water and ether, are disposed, ten in a column, the fifty letters of the alphabet including some supplementary signs. When the first letter of the neophyte's name corresponds to the first letter of the *mantra*, this may be revealed, but, otherwise, there must be taken into account the relation of friendship or opposition which exists between the different elements and therefore between the name of the neophyte and that of the divinity, set out respectively in individual groups. For instance, earth and wind, fire and wind, are friends, but water is the enemy of fire and so also is earth of fire. The ether is always friendly. (*Tantrasāra*, p. 9)

When, by the means we have described, the officiant is assured as to the efficacy of the rite, he can proceed to the decisive phase of the initiatory ritual, that is to say to the descent of the divine force, of the various *numina* represented on the *maṇḍala*, so that this is no longer an inert plan but is transformed into a living cosmos, including within itself the divine forces whose symbols represent them in a form which is comprehensible to the human intellect. This is accomplished by the *āvahana* rite (which I have referred to several times above) that brings about the descent of the *numen* into the officiant. This descent takes place in two distinct phases which are designated by the technical terms *samayasattva* and *jñānasattva*.

Here we have one of the most important phases of gnostic evocation and one of the most difficult to understand, but it will become clearer when we have translated the entire description of an evocatory rite in which the two aspects, temporal or conventional being (*samayasattva*) and ideal being (*jñānasattva*), are so contrasted that a definition of both of them appears more easy. We have a *sādhana*—a liturgical formula—and a Yoga exercise intended to evoke Khasarpana, one of the many forms of Avalokiteśvara, the God of Compassion:

'When, after the ceremony and the prescribed meditation, the image of the God has been visualized in front of the initiate (this moment is called in Tibetan *mdun bskyed* "the producing of the image before one") the *sādhaka* will imagine himself as identical with that God, imagining upon the head of his own body (thus ideally identified with Khasarpana) the syllable OṂ, on his neck the syllable AḤ, on his heart the syllable HŪṂ, each one of them set upon a lotus flower. With this method he may meditate as long as he may desire.

'Then there emanate from the syllable HŪṂ infinite reflections of the splendid lunar rays which disperse the darkness of ignorance in the three kinds of worlds (infernal, terrestrial and divine). This syllable HŪṂ is the mystical seed of the God, white like an autumnal lotus emerging from the immaculate disk of the moon, visualized as the heart of this *samayasattva* which has the aspect of Lokanātha (Khasarpana). These rays attract from the most remote worlds the same God in the *jñānasattva* form which exists *ab aeterno*. When he has thus led to himself (transformed into *samayasattva*) this God, the initiate should think of him standing before him and mentally should wash the feet of Lokanātha (thus appearing in the form of *jñānasattva*) with water drawn from a vase adorned with various gems, and he should honour this God (in the aspect of *jñānasattva*) with exoteric and esoteric ritual of various sorts: flowers, incense, lamps, vestments, umbrellas, flags, bells and standards, all of celestial quality. When he has thus repeatedly done honour to the God, he should pronounce four syllables: JAḤ, KUṂ, VAṂ, BO and should place his hands in the "seal" called *vikasitakamalamudrā*[1] "the seal of the lotus in bloom". When, by virtue of this seal, he has led the God to him, he should think of him in that aspect and by pronouncing OṂ, AḤ, HŪṂ, he should recognize in this God (who has the appearance of *samayasattva* and is identical with the initiate himself) the non-duality of the two aspects, *samayasattva* and *jñānasattva*.'

Samaya means in Sanskrit 'convention', 'rule',[2] 'vow' and *sattva* signifies 'being', 'creature'. The *samayasattva*, then, is a 'conventional being' provisionally provoked by certain rules assumed by the meditator who is, ideally, transfigured into the divinity on to whom he has concentrated his mind. When he has evoked the image of the God before him, the initiate lives on another plane, beyond *saṃsāra*, where the laws of *māyā* operate. It is clear from this that his transformation is provisional, a temporary adaptation to the spiritual reality symbolized by the deity, but it is necessary since the God thus invoked dwells in him. And so between the plane of *saṃsāra* and that of the archetypes there must be provisionally a link or meeting point, and this is the function of the *samayasattva*, the momentary transfiguration of the meditator by the essence of the God which is transferred into him.

When the *samayasattva* condition has been brought about, then the *jñānasattva*, the 'projection' of the God (which cor-

[1] The *mudrā* called 'seal' is the particular attitude of the hands which accompanies the *mantra* or invocation of the divinity or which causes to reach the divinity the formula which is addressed to him.

[2] Many esoteric rules are quoted in *Guhyasamāja*, p. 127 ff.

responds to an essential archetype existing *ab aeterno*), descends into this regenerated being who has offered to the God all kinds of honour and worship. The 'projection' of the God there takes up its abode. The *samayasattva* merges with the *jñānasattva* and so is brought about a substitution of nature, a replacement of the *saṃsāra* appearance by the archetypal essence.

Such a manifestation in the heart of the officiant might seem, at first sight, a discordant phase in the harmonious system we have described and which appears to us as a process of ascent from the multiple to the One, of reconstitution of the original Unity, beyond the world of appearances in which we find ourselves fallen and immersed. In the case of the *samaysattva* and of the *jñānasattva* we seem to witness a descent as though a ray of light came down from on high, although only provisionally, and filled us and transformed us. But this is, so to speak, an error of perspective, since we have that light within us, it does not descend upon, but reveals itself to, us. The *jñānasattva* which lights up within our hearts, indicates the awakening of cognition which is introduced, with suitable symbols, into the psyche and can only thus take up its abode there. It then substitutes its own luminous image for those which previously rioted therein, and by gathering around itself, as in a central fire, the attention of the subject, it prevents the distractions and appeals of the outside world.

In any case, the descent of the *jñānasattva* is a decisive moment in the process of revulsion, inasmuch as, in an individual still subject to *saṃsāra*, a new state is determined at that instant. By this he finds himself on another plane, on that of consciousness, upon which are projected the symbols of the Gods expressed in the *maṇḍala*. This is not yet the supercosmic state, but one in which merely illuminated cognition takes possession, with its symbols, of the psyche and substitutes itself for them. At this moment, the initiate, by the concentration of his mind, takes part, as actor, in the supreme consecration which will impose a definitive seal on his rebirth. The baptism given him by the Master will then be replaced by an ideal one in which the Buddhas, coming from all parts of space, will consecrate his palingenesis, the revulsion which has taken place and by which consciousness that was refracted, lost and dissipated in time and space, has become, once again, one and luminous. And the Buddhas not only baptize him but, miraculously, are reabsorbed into him then to emanate from him in their luminous forms. Thus is repeated the in-and-out breath of things which takes place eternally and in which, by our regained cognition, instead of being spectators we act. The mystic identifies himself with Vajrasattva, finding himself in the centre of the supercosmic *maṇḍala* which is the *raison d'être* of the whole cosmos, its source and the place to which it returns. Because of this correspondence between the macrocosm and the microcosm—which we have mentioned several times—the paradigm of this transposition of the *maṇḍala* into the initiate reproduces the autogenous primordial creation which drew from the Undefined, filled full of infinite possibilities, all that is apparent. At that moment the world was born from that archetypal structure which the Supreme One contained within himself and which, after the cycles of the ages, he will one day take back again into himself. It is a stupendous process that develops through successive emanations from the *maṇḍala* which, from the most subtle and impenetrable, progressively pass into the visible and concrete.

It is enough to recall the first chapter of the *Guhyasamāja* (interpreted by the aid of Candrakīrti) in which this *maṇḍala* procession is evoked in its entirety starting from the initial moment when in the immensity of the void Vajradhara the Blessed absorbs into his diamond essence the infinite number of Buddhas and Bodhisattvas who with him peopled the void and filled it like sesame seeds, only to project them out again into the *maṇḍala*—(Vajradhara who bears the *vajra* dwells in the wombs of the diamond women together with the essence of the three planes of spirit, word and body which compose the All). The archetypal forms then multiply gradually, in a continuous process of absorption and of luminous emanations, provoked, from time to time, by various states of concentration (*samādhi*) in a dichotomy of males and females and then by essenced modes which govern the mechanism of the universe. And all the powers thus emanated into the huge *maṇḍala* which fills the infinity of space constitute the eternal form and the indefectible structure of the universe.

(I) (A) 'At one time the Blessed One was in the womb of the adamantine women (that is of the powers) which constitute the essence of the physical, verbal and spiritual plane of all the Tathāgatas (realizing, that is to say, the synthesis of the void of the beatitude) together with countless Bodhisattvas and Mahāsattvas of ineffable numbers, as many as the specks of dust in all the Sumeru mountains (axes of the innumerable worlds each one of which is protected by a Buddha), that is, The Bodhisattva Mahāsattva, Diamond Rule (Sarvāvaranaviskāmbin, emanation of Akṣobhya), Diamond Body (Kṣitigarbha, emanation of Vairocana), Diamond Word (Lokeśvara, emanation of Amitābha), Diamond Thought (Vajrapāṇi, emanation of Akṣobhya), Diamond Concentration (Akāśagarbha, emanation of Ratnasaṃbhava), Diamond Victory (*jaya* instead of *jāpa* of the text, and Maitreya, emanation of Amoghasiddhi). Then,

(B) 'The female Bodhisattvas, Earth Diamond (Locana, counterpart of Vairocana), Diamond Water (Māmakī, counterpart of Ratnasaṃbhava), Diamond Fire (Pāṇḍaravasinī, counterpart of Amitābha), Diamond Wind (Samayatārā, counterpart of Amoghasiddhi) and Diamond Ether (Mañjuśrī). Then,

(C) 'The Diamonds of Materiality, Sound, Perfume, Taste and Touch. Then,

(D) 'The Diamond of the plane of the Law (Samantabhadra) and with the following five Diamond Tathāgatas: Akṣobhya, Vairocana, Ratneketu, Amitābha and Amogha. And all space appeared as a sesame seed, full of Tathāgatas, beginning with those which throng all space.

(II) 'Then the Blessed Mahāvairocana (that is Vajradhara) plunged into the concentration called "Of the Diamond of the Great Passion of the Tathāgatas" and made all the Tathāgatas enter the three diamonds of his body, word and spirit. Then these Tathāgatas in order to please the Blessed Lord of the body, word and spirit of all the Tathāgatas, made by artifice, their own bodies to assume the appearance of women and thus they issued from the body of the blessed Vairocana.

'Some of them took on the form of Buddhalocanī, others that of Samayatārā, or Pāṇḍaravasinī; some took on the form of the Diamond of materiality, others the forms of the Diamonds of sound, perfume, or touch (that is to say four counterparts corresponding to the four Tathāgatas situated in the four points of space, excluding the central deity of the *maṇḍala*, the immobile centre operating through the activity of his emanation projected towards descent in time and space).

(III) 'Then the Tathāgata Akṣobhya (in other words Vajradhara who a little earlier was called Mahāvairocana) in the wombs of the diamond women constituting the essence of the physical, verbal and spiritual plane of the Buddha, sustained with his grace the *maṇḍala* of the great rule (*samaya*) splendid (that is solar), pure, given essence by him (that is, his reflection) of a different appearance in each part, strewn with clouds of Buddhas, flaming with fiery particles (the ten wrathful deities who surround the *maṇḍala*), the city of all the Tathāgatas united with the pure *maṇḍala*, etc.

'Then the Blessed One (Vajradhara), Lord of the Diamond of body, word and spirit of the Tathāgatas, took up his place[1] at the centre of the *maṇḍala* of all the Tathāgatas and then the Tathāgatas Akṣobhya, Ratnaketu, Amitāyuḥ, Amoghasiddi and Vairocana, found themselves in the heart of the Tathāgata Bodhicittavajra (Diamond of the Thought of Illumination, Absolute Essence, Vajradhara, the Centre and First Principle in which through the commotion which occurred and which is described in the preceding phase, the pentad is brought about).

(IV) 'Then the Blessed Bodhicittavajra plunged into the concentration called that of the "Diamond of the Lordship of all the Tathāgatas" and at once the sphere of space became full of the Diamond of all the Tathāgatas. And then the creatures which were in all spheres of space, by virtue of the grace of Vajrasattva, became participants in the beatitude and serenity peculiar to all the Tathāgatas.

(V) 'Then the Tathāgata Bodhicittavajra plunged into the concentration called the "Diamond of the Germination of the Rule of the Diamond of the body, word and spirit of all the Tathāgatas" and conferred the sustaining grace, the essence of all Tathāgatas, on the form of the man (that is Tathāgata) of the great wisdom[2] (*Mantra: oṃ ā hūṃ*). As soon as this grace had been bestowed the Blessed Bodhicittavajra was seen with threefold face (that is the three letters *Oṃ ā hūṃ*) by all the Tathāgatas.

'(Then all the Tathāgatas, beginning with Akṣobhya who had been emanated from the heart of Bodhicittavajra, requested, with different invocations, Bodhicittavajra to reveal what truth may be and how it may be attained.)

(VI) 'Then the Blessed One, the Tathāgata Sarvatathāgatakāyavagcittavajra, taking notice of this prayer of all the

[1] *pratiṣṭhāpayāmāsa*, i.e. *ātmānam*.

[2] mahāvidyā; here vidyā, should be intended as a secret formula, or mantra, impregnated with unimpeded magic efficacy: the *vidyāpuruṣa* is the man who possesses that vidyā.

Tathāgatas, plunged into the concentration called "Diamond of the Torch of Knowledge" (of non-duality) and as soon as he was plunged in this, from the three Diamonds of his own body, word and spirit, he emitted the heart[1] of the supreme essence of the family of hatred—*vajradhṛk.*

'As soon as this (heart) was pronounced, this Blessed One, man of wisdom, made up of the body, word and spirit of all the Tathāgatas (Mahāvajradhara) sat down[2] in the Diamond of the body, word and spirit of all the Tathāgatas in black, white and red form, by means of the supreme syllables of the conjunction with the seal of Akṣobhya (that is, participating in the essential nature of the One, there projects from himself, in virtue of this formula, a three-fold plane corresponding to the symbol of Akṣobhya—hatred—and this places itself in the *maṇḍala*).

(VIII) 'Then the Blessed One plunged into the concentration called "Diamond of Germination of the Convention" (*samaya*) and emitted from the Diamond of his own body, word and spirit, the heart of the supreme essence of the family of mental perturbation *jinajik.* As soon as this (heart) was pronounced, this Blessed One, man of wisdom of the body, word and spirit of all the Tathāgatas, sat down before the "Diamond of the body, word and spirit of all the Tathāgatas" in the white, black and red form by means of the supreme syllable of the conjunction with the seal of Vairocana.

'Then, the Blessed One, having plunged into the concentration called the "Glory of the Diamond of the Generation of the Jewel of all the Tathāgatas", emitted from the Diamond of the body, word and spirit the heart of the supreme essence of the family of the jewel, *ratnadhṛk.* As soon as this (heart) had been pronounced, this Blessed One, man

[1] *hṛdaya* is heart: that is the quintessence of a thing, a formula, which condenses a truth, or expresses the essential meaning of a doctrine.

[2] Here also the causative has for object atmānan: made himself sit down, sat down.

of wisdom of the Diamond of body, word and spirit of all the Tathāgatas, sat down at the right of the "Diamond of the body, word and spirit of all the Tathāgatas" in the yellow, white and black form, by means of the supreme syllables of the conjunction with the seal of Ratnaketu.

'Then, the Blessed One having plunged into the concentration called the "Diamond of the Germination of the Great Passion of all the Tathāgatas" emitted from the Diamond of the body, word and spirit the heart of the supreme essence of the family of the adamantine passion: *ārolik*. As soon as this (heart) had been pronounced, this Blessed One, man of the wisdom of the body, word and spirit of all the Tathāgatas sat down at the left of the "Diamond of the body word and spirit of all the Tathāgatas" in the red, white and black form, by means of the supreme syllables of the conjunction with the great seal of Lokeśvara, Lord of Great Wisdom.

'Then the Blessed One plunged into the concentration called the "Diamond of the Germination of the Infallible Convention" (*samaya*) of all the Tathāgatas and emitted from the threefold diamond of his own body, word and spirit, the heart of the supreme essence of the family that attracts the secret (*samaya:* the light, *odgsal*, *prajñadhṛk*. As soon as this (heart) had been pronounced, the Blessed One, man of the wisdom of the body, word and spirit of all the Tathāgatas, seated himself at the north of the "Diamond of the body, word and spirit" in the yellow, white and black form by means of the supreme syllable of the conjunction with the great seal of Amoghavajra.

'Of hatred (Akṣobhya), of mental perturbation (Vairocana), of passion (Amitābha), of the gem (Ratnaketu), of the convention (*samaya*) (Amoghasiddhi), of these are the five families which carry on to the fulfilment of love and salvation.

(VIII) 'Then the Blessed One plunged into the concentration called "The Convention (*samaya*) that gratifies (*anurāgaṇa*) the Keeper of the Diamond of all the Tathāgatas" (that is Akṣobhya) and emitted from the threefold diamond of the body, the word and the spirit, the Supreme Consort of the Keeper of all the Diamonds: *dveṣarati* (hatred-pleasure).

'As soon as this was emitted, the Blessed One, man of wisdom of the body, word and spirit of all the Tathāgatas, assumed the appearance of a woman and seated himself in the "Diamond of the body, word and spirit of all the Tathāgatas".

'Then the Blessed One plunged into the concentration called "The Diamond that Gratifies (*anurāgaṇa*) all the Tathāgatas" (Amitābha) and from the threefold Diamond of his own body, word and spirit emitted the supreme Consort of all the Tathāgatas (Vairocana); *moharati* (mental perturbation-pleasure).

'As soon as this was emitted, the Blessed One etc. . . . assumed the appearance of a woman and seated himself in the eastern corner.

'Then the Blessed One plunged into the concentration called the "Diamond that Gratifies (*anurāgaṇa*) the Keepers of Passion of all the Tathāgatas" (Amitābha) and from the threefold Diamond etc. emitted the Supreme Consort of the Keeper of Passions: *rāgarati* (passion-pleasure).

'As soon as the Blessed One etc. . . . assumed the aspect of a woman and seated himself in the western corner.

'Then the Blessed One plunged into the concentration called "The Diamond of the non-contradiction of the body, word and spirit of all the Tathāgatas" (Amoghasiddhi) and from the threefold Diamond etc. he emitted the Supreme Consort of the Keeper of the gnosis of the Tathāgatas, *vajrarati* (diamond-pleasure).

'As soon as the Blessed One etc. . . . assumed the aspect of a woman and seated himself in the northern corner.

'Then the Blessed One plunged into the concentration

called "The Diamond of Mahāvairocana" and from the threefold Diamond etc. emitted the Mahākrodha, sustaining power of the *maṇḍala* of all the Tathāgatas: *Yamantakṛt* ("he who destroys Yama"—Yama is *avidyā*, ignorance).

'As soon as the Blessed One etc. . . . in the form that terrifies all the Tathāgatas seated himself in the eastern gate.

'Then the Blessed One plunged into the concentration called "the Diamond of the Illumination of all the Tathāgatas" and emitted etc. the Mahākrodha, sustaining power of the *maṇḍala* of the Keeper of the Passion of all the Tathāgatas; *prajñāntakṛt.*

'As soon as the Blessed One etc. . . . in a form that terrifies all the adamantine convention, seated himself in the southern gate.

'Then the Blessed One plunged into the concentration called "The Diamond that Dominates the Law of all the Tathāgatas" and emitted etc. the Mahākrodha, sustaining power of the *maṇḍala* of the Keeper of the Passion of all the Tathāgatas; *padmāntakṛt.*

'As soon as etc. . . . in the form of the voice of all the Tathāgatas he seated himself on the western gate.

'Then the Blessed One plunged into the meditation called "The Diamond of the body, of the word and of the spirit of all the Tathāgatas" and emitted the Mahākrodha, sustaining power of the *maṇḍala* of the body, word and spirit of all the Tathāgatas: *Vighnāntakṛt.*

'As soon as etc. . . . in the form of the body, word and spirit of all the Tathāgatas, he seated himself on the northern gate.'

From this model, as has been said above, the meditator starts, by identifying himself with the Supreme Essence, represented by the symbol he selects and thus becomes reintegrated into the One—All. If his concentration is not interrupted, in the centre of his own heart, the matrix of all things that can be created, he will see the syllable HŪṂ light up and from its incandescence he will see emanating the infinite number of divine forms which place themselves round about him, according to the plan of the *maṇḍala.* They then reabsorb themselves in him, thus renewing the primordial drama. The mystic, consubstantiated with the One Being, is transported outside time at that moment. He can then substitute for these visualized forms the more subtle structure of the *maṇḍala,* which, instead of such images, presents the *mantras* or geminal formulae of the Universal Essence.

As I have said above, this baptism, a description of which is given in the first pages of a celebrated book on Indian gnosis, does not take place just once as at the beginning of the cosmic creation. It is rather an epiphany, a manifestation which appears to the initiate when at the end of his spiritual preparation he comes to be identified with the centre of the *maṇḍala,* the point from which all goes forth and to which all returns and from where the archetypal essences stream forth in luminous rays which pervade the whole world, arousing it from nothing and reabsorbing it. From the spirit of the mystic who is absorbed in the contemplation which transports him on to the plane of eternal existence, there blaze forth, shining round about, the divine matrices of things. He sees them issue from him and re-enter him in that symbol which religious experience has fixed in definite forms. Only thus can he imagine himself as the actor in the cosmic drama and from the experience of life rise up once more to the Origin. The images that the mystic sees come forth from the centre of his own heart pervade space and then reabsorb themselves in him. They deify him and almost burn him with their lightning flashes. They are not inert and insignificant images. They calm the stormy sea of the subconscious and they illuminate his darkness. The soul's discord is extinguished and on to its agitation there dawns a steady and serene light.

Thus, the reading of the *maṇḍala*, the reliving in one's own consciousness of the phases which the *maṇḍala* represents, the spiritual and orderly progression through the various stages that are shown, symbolically, upon its surface induces a deliverance, a lusis. Little by little the neophyte arrives at the central point by passing gradually from one sector to another of the *maṇḍala* (that is from one interior state to a following one that is more complete, which does not annul the preceding one but overcomes it by including it in itself). This may take place literally, as with the great *maṇḍalas* adopted in initiation ceremonies when the mystic, after having passed through the different parts of the *maṇḍala*, finds himself physically present at the centre and so experiences the *maṇḍala*'s catharsis in himself. Or it may occur mentally when by concentrating his mind on the pattern of the *maṇḍala* he realizes in himself the truth which this pattern typifies. Naturally this central point is the fifth, the last one susceptible of being represented visibly. Beyond and above is the sixth point, the other plane, the Vajradhara, the Absolute, in which the mystic is annihilated by penetrating into its luminosity with a revulsion of plane that occurs suddenly and immediately from the centre of the *maṇḍala* when it has been reached. The revulsion is the matter of one instant: when one has entered the divine truth or essence even for a moment, one has known everything (*Īśvarapratyabhijñāvimarśinī of Abhinavagupta*, vol. III, p. 407, v. 10).

Therefore, the process reveals itself to the eyes of the mystic who has been duly initiated as an immense mobile *maṇḍala* which now stands out in the splendour of its visible symbols—the resplendent and dazzling images of Gods aureoled with celestial glories—and then, again, is absorbed into the central point, the immobile star which gathers all into itself and from which emanates everything in turn. But he is, ideally, that centre and he identifies the mystical lotus on the top of his head with the point that is the inexhaustible matrix of all that is, that was and that shall be.

We are, thus, led, necessarily, to speak of this supreme phase, of this transference of the *maṇḍala* into the mystic's own body.

5

THE MAṆḌALA IN THE HUMAN BODY

WITH the passage of the centuries both Buddhism and Hinduism accentuated the psychological introspection we meet with at the very dawn of Indian religious life. On to the *maṇḍala* was projected the drama of cosmic disintegration and reintegration as relived by the individual, sole contriver of his own salvation, that is to say of his return to the *logos spermatikos*.

But although the individual lives this drama, experiences it and enjoys its fruits, is it not perhaps possible to do without the *maṇḍala* and to situate in the individual himself the symbolism which it represents? The transition was facilitated by the correspondence between the macrocosm and the microcosm, a correspondence which is the fundamental proposition of Yoga and which is accepted by the gnostic sects of India and not of India alone. Not only is the body analogous to the universe, in its physical extent and divisions; but it also contains within itself all the Gods (*sarve devāḥ ṣarīrasthāḥ*, *Guptadikṣātantra*, quoted in *Śāktānandataraṅginī*, p. 31: for the correspondence between world and body, see ibid, p. 9).

So, the external *maṇḍala* is transferred to the internal *maṇḍala*, namely to the body in which the same symbols as those of the former are placed in similar arrangement. The ideal centre of the *maṇḍala* is the *brahmarandhra*, the 'cavity of Brahmā' at the top of the head where there debouches the *suṣūmnā*, the median canal which, along the spinal column, traverses the human body from the perineum to the top of the head. In cosmic correspondence this column is Sumeru, the central mountain of the universe on whose flanks are disposed the various celestial planes, just as in the human body the various centres are differentiated by wheels (*cakra*), the inevitable phases in the process of reintegration.

As beyond the summit of Sumeru there extends infinite space, symbol of the other plane, that of non-*saṃsāra* or *nirvāṇa*, so, also, when reintegration has been brought about, and illusory identity is suppressed, the unknown is dissolved *ipso facto* into the purity of the cosmic Consciousness which transcends the personality.

The psychic life of the individual reflects that of the universe. We are, essentially, illumination, *bodhi* and *dharma-kāya*, of 'Buddha essence', says the Buddhist and 'supreme Consciousness' (*paramā-samvit*), that is Śiva, assert the Śaivites, but we are its opposite, or, better, its limit. In us is reproduced, from instant to instant, the same process which that primeval light directs to individualization. The force of thought that flows through five stages and phases of varied luminosity from the perineum to the *brahmarandhra*, there to be reintegrated, is imagined as a luminous point, equivalent to that primeval Light, that uncreated and eternal Origin of all things. This is in the centre of the individual just as the symbol of the first principle is in the centre of the *maṇḍala*. It is the instant point in which is contained the infinite and the eternal. In the process of evocation when the mystic has entered into a state of concentration (*samādhi*) and has escaped from this plane and becomes identified with the cosmic Consciousness in its creative phase, there are projected from his own germinal thought, from the seeds which the contemplative imagines deposited or described within him, those bands of coloured light which express the first quivering or inequality of the originally motionless luminosity of

Consciousness. These are visualized in the form of the five Tathāgatas or of the first five aspects of Śiva.

The contemplative sees them stream out from the secret depths of his being and place themselves in the lotus of his heart. Just as above the *maṇḍala*, invisible but omnipresent, there is *Vajradhara*, the starting-point, preceding all dichotomic process, and yet a necessary condition of it, so, also in the man-*maṇḍala*, this supreme point which both conditions and transcends his infinite radiations, is outside the body, high above the *brahmarandhra*.

But how does reintegration, induced by concentration on the man-*maṇḍala*, take place? In the process we are considering now, the mystic knows that the principle of salvation is within him. He knows, also, that this principle will remain inert if he does not, with all his strength, seek it, find it and make it active.

On the way of redemption, to which he has devoted himself, he has need of all his will-power and vigilance in order to put in motion the forces of his own psyche so that it, which keeps him bound, may furnish him, none the less, with the means of salvation provided that he knows how to penetrate into his psyche and to subdue it. The body, with its demands and its allurements, represents for the non-initiated the first coefficient of *karmic* accumulation. It is the effect, but at the same time the instrument, of *avidyā*, of nescience. The body demands to be looked after, to be satisfied, to be favoured in its desires. It is the vehicle of emanation, the basis of affective life. But, at the same time, without this body we could not enjoy the beauty of things, not catch that first glimmer of divine omnipotence which is displayed in the magnificence of nature. Indeed, if tamed by a suitable discipline, the psycho-physical complex will be directed towards new possibilities. In order to effect this, the initiate has recourse to Yoga, and especially to *Haṭhayoga*. He does not deny the body but he uses it as a necessary instrument of salvation. 'The essence of all things is in our bodies, when thou shalt know thy own body, thy own foundation is firm.' (*Amṛtaratnāvalī*)

The body corresponds to what the Tibetans, in the terminology of the *maṇḍala*, call the *rten* (in Sanskrit *ādhāra*), that is the physical support of the divine effulgence. The body is like a vessel born of the very operation of those divine forces which dwell within it and which with their manifestation determine expansion in space and succession in time. Therefore, the body is not a contemptible aggregate of corruptible substance, nor a painful and impure envelope (as the mystical literature of Hinduist and Buddhist Schools is never tired of repeating and so of inculcating into men's souls a bitter contempt of the world), but a sacred instrument in virtue of which Man, if he knows how to use it, may save himself. Thus the body is given its full importance in the gnostic Schools. Without a healthy body there could be no practice of *Haṭhayoga* which is a certain means of prompt salvation, a swift path by which is brought about violently (*haṭha*) the revulsion from the plane of *saṃsāra* to that of the *nirvāṇa*. 'Without the body Man can obtain no result.' (*Rudrayāmala*, I, v. 160)

'If we had no body how could there be beatitude?' (*Hevajratantra*, 24, a). 'An incorporeal being lies hidden in the body, whosoever is cognizant of its presence there, is liberated.' (*Doha* of Saraha, 13)

The body is like a boat in which Man, plying the oar of the purified mind, passes to the other shore of the sea of existence. 'Act in such a way that the five Buddhas may become the five oars and with all thy strength tear away the veils of illusion.' (*Doha* of Kanha, 38)

Thus the two worlds, the physical and the spiritual, are not irremediably opposed, but, acting through the medium of the psyche, both the one and the other co-operate to redemption, indissoluble, in the living unity of the individual.

Indeed, and this is one of the essential points of Indian experience, reintegration is a fruit of this life. There is no need to die in order to be reunited, once more, with the first Principle. Reintegration, once it has been accomplished, is a positive fact and there can be no lapsing therefrom. Thus a Bodhisattva, when he attains the seventh land, the tenth stage of the spiritual ascent which he must effect, is *avinivarttanīya*, he never turns back again. He is healed, he has overcome his psyche in an absolute fashion and he can no more return to the agitation of the psyche, as the victim of its passion and the slave of *karma*.

When such a Bodhisattva gains Illumination he becomes a Buddha. He enters into *nirvāṇa*. He is *nirvṛta*. That is to say the grip of the psyche is shaken off for ever. He is on the other plane, on the plane of the Real which transcends *avidyā*, *māyā* and *karma*. Death is of no avail for the acquisition of palingenesis. Death, for him who has realized the supreme experience, is *parinirvāṇa*, the absolute *nirvāṇa*, inasmuch as the body no longer exists, and the body, by the mere fact of its existence, gathers together within itself the inviolable *karmic* experiences of the past, but in this maturity loosens and eliminates them.

Parinirvāṇa, with the 'leap' already accomplished on to the other plane, marks the absolute end of the process of *karma* and also of that process which is actuated by extinction, the arrest of all projection into the plane of *saṃsāra*. But *parinirvāṇa* adds nothing to that which, as it is an absolute condition, is not susceptible of completion, or of modification. Such, in any case, is the contention of the Śaiva School.

But how can I, an unstable creature, lapsed in time and at any moment liable to perish, perceive, written and designed in myself, the scheme of the eternal flux of things and, above all, how can I discover within myself the light after which I seek? How can I merge myself in it once more?

At this point, we must call to mind the psychophysics of *Haṭhayoga.* This conceived of the body as traversed by an infinite number of canals (*nāḍi*) among which three are the most important, the *iḍā* or *lalanā* to the left, the *piṅgalā* or *rasanā* to the right and the *caṇḍālī*, *avadhūti* or *suṣumnā* in the middle. Through the first two there runs *prāṇa*, or vital energy, identified, generally, with breath or respiration, which is the vehicle on which is carried *citta*, namely, the principle of the psyche's volitive, affective and intellective activity. *Citta*, drawn along in these two canals by *prāṇa*, is always active and lively, puts us into contact with the outer world and brings to us the world's voices and impressions. *Citta* reacts in a thousand different ways and thus waves the net which keeps us in prison with external things, and tends always to carry us outside ourselves. The aim of Yoga is to cause the restless and unstable *citta* to flow back through the two veins which run respectively from the right and left nostril and meet at the perineum, into the *caṇḍālī*, namely the median canal which is thought of as running along the spinal column from the perineum to the *brahmarandhra* at the sagittal suture of the head. In this *caṇḍālī* is present, or reflected, the cosmic Consciousness, the first Principle, Illumination, the essential *bodhi*. *Haṭhayoga* causes a violent arrest (*haṭha*) of the *citta's* movement and it becomes immobile in the *caṇḍālī* where it flares up. From this fire is released illumination and consciousness is reinstated. The reintegration is accomplished in three distinct phases, localized, according to Buddhism, in three wheels (*cakra*), disposed in three different parts of the body and which are assimilated to the three bodies of the Buddha (see Fig. 1). The *citta* gradually becomes purified until it ceases all activity and vanishes in the supreme beatitude of the *sahaja*, the absolute Principle immanent in us.

The road to reintegration of the Śaiva Schools is a longer one but it is substantially the same. The 'wheels' through which the *citta* must travel on its ascent to the primordial Man-Woman are five instead of three. Of course, the *sahasrāra* and the *uṣṇīṣakamala*, the 'Lotus of a thousand petals', on the summit of the head, the Man-Woman, the Absolute is outside time and space and, therefore, is not counted among the 'wheels'. It is on the other plane. An active force governs this alternate and eternal movement of descent and of expansion from the One to the All, and conversely, of return or ascent from the All to the One. This force is the *upāya*, the 'means', the 'compassion' (*karuṇā*), of the Buddhist Schools, and the *śakti* of the Śaiva, according to the different stress which the one or the other of these Schools lays on the masculine or feminine aspect of the uncreated Man-Woman.

The primordial union, moved by an inevitable interior impulse to multiply itself, splits into two. It is the reversed triangle, symbol of the power (*śakti*) which, although indissolubly joined to the Absolute, nevertheless, gives the illusion of being separated from it, in order to create the world as far as the extreme limit of the *caṇḍālī*. There this power falls asleep, and coiling itself like a serpent shuts this canal into which the individuated principle must enter in order to recover liberating consciousness and to undertake the way of return and the reabsorption of itself into the One. We would recall, at this point, what has been said above concerning the five aspects of Śiva and about the manifestation of the force of *māyā*. The lower extremity of the *caṇḍālī* marks another 'leap' which is accomplished in the evolutive process. The first took place when, on the immobile surface of the Real, there manifested the first quivering which led to the refraction of the Indivisible One in the pentad. These colorations, if we may adopt this spatial expression, for a being that is outside space, remain on the same level. The eruption of *māyā* is the second 'leap' and with this comes the fall into individuation. Then comes the upsurge of the individual soul (*puruṣa*) and of the psycho-physical complex (*prakṛti*) objectivity and duality. On this threshold is *kuṇḍalinī*, the *śakti* asleep in the lower orifice of the *caṇḍālī*.

The thorax contains the five wheels, the archetypes, over which rises the lotus with a thousand petals. Below *kuṇḍalinī* the multiplication of duality is due to the ever-increasing darkening of consciousness, which does not recognize itself any more in things and does not perceive that these are reflections, whence it is agitated and drowns itself in the illusion of a non-Ego. Thus, the *śakti*, active but intelligent force, the *cit-śakti* of Śiva, the primordial female, is no longer illuminated by its own light, but asleep and inert it shuts the way of Return. This intelligent force, now torpid and drowsy, is no longer capable of being itself again and of re-ascending to its real place to merge itself into complete co-existence with Śiva. The sleeping *kuṇḍalinī* marks the stopping-point, the phase which indicates the distance between the two planes. Here begins the state of vigil (*jāgrat*), when the psyche clings to the world which, by its ways, entices and decoys us. But our vigil is the slumber of the divine intelligence, its drowsiness. *Haṭhayoga* must induce awakening. *Kuṇḍalinī*, then aroused from its torpor, declares itself, tends to reconstitute the primordial Man-Woman and is therefore represented by a triangle with the apex upwards. It is the ascent which is laboriously accomplished from wheel to wheel up to the *sahasrāra*, the lotus of a thousand petals. Each wheel is a new increase of consciousness, one of the five *śakti* which becomes illuminated. After the fifth stage all five are fused into the unique and sole *Śakti* which receives them into itself. Thus reintegrated, the *Śakti* rises up to the *sahasrāra*, restored to the transcendent Unity.

In this intuition of *Haṭhayoga*, in this imagined palingenesis of the initiate—transformed into a mystical *maṇḍala* in which the world flux is repeated—there flow together the most ancient experiences of an India always disposed to transmute primitive cosmic correspondences into psychical relations.

In the Ṛg Veda we find a ternary division of the world into *bhūḥ*, *bhuvaḥ*, *svaḥ*, that is earth, atmospheric space and heaven, created by three appropriate words, the sounds pronounced by *Vāc*, the Word. But this ternary division was quickly transformed into a quaternary series, since beyond the sky (*svarga*) is the luminous space in which, at times, appears the celestial eye, the Sun. In the same manner, as we have seen, the central Asiatic nomads conceived the world as a tent from whose central orifice (on which is posed the axis of the world) there streams down the light of sidereal space, which is above the atmosphere, the boundary between that which has form and that which has no form, that which is subject to time and that which stands above time. This is the Brahman of India, *bhūtakoṭi*, the summit of all existence, according to Buddhist cosmology. Beyond is dharmakāya, the uncreated (*asaṃskṛta*), the changeless Principle and Cause of all that change. It is symbolized by three-quarters of a column (or of the inverted cosmic tree). One quarter is the world of things while the other three are fixed and immobile, being the base from which all is derived and the sixteenth unalterable phase (*tithi*) of the moon, the totality of things in their changeless archetype. In the speculations of some later gnostic Schools this sixteenth lunar day is motionless and causes the succession of the moon's phases. For them, therefore, it symbolizes the continuous flowing out and reabsorption of the divine forces, the *śakti* in the alternating play of cosmic evolution and involution. In this adaptation of the macrocosm to the microcosm, by which the latter is made a synthesis of the universe, three centres correspond to *bhūḥ*, *bhuvaḥ* and *svaḥ* (earth, atmosphere, sky) and by rising successively through these, consciousness is reintegrated in its primitive unity. These three centres are the sexual organs, the heart and the brain, and on the top of the head the *brahmarandhra*, the 'orifice of Brahma' from beyond which is accomplished the 'leap' into the other sphere.

When it is transposed into the world of consciousness the tetrad assumes a more complex value. To the first three phases correspond, respectively, the state of vigil (*jāgrat*) when consciousness is active in the world, the state of sleep (*svapna*) in which consciousness is not disturbed by sensations but only by images, and, lastly, the state of profound sleep in which all impressions lie lulled but ready to awaken when this state of serenity ceases.

But above these three states is *turīya*, the fourth state, that is consciousness reintegrated in all its purity.

Creation of the word in three sounds	*Macrocosm* *Brahman*	*Microcosm* *brahma-randhra*	*Psychical states* *turīya*	*bhūtakoṭi*
svaḥ *bhuvaḥ* *bhūḥ*	*svaḥ* *bhuvaḥ* *bhūḥ*	brain heart sexual organs	*suṣupti* *svapna* *jāgrat*	

The same quadruple process from the One to the many and inversely of the return from the many to the One is adapted by the Śaiva Schools for expressing the idea of the Word. This process is accomplished, says Abhinavagupta, in four phases, by which the absolute and indiscriminate consciousness incorporates itself into the concrete form of a particular idea expressed by the corresponding word. As sublime (*parā*) this is supreme Consciousness, absolute potentiality, anterior to all separation (into two). Thus, in ourselves, sound (*nāḍa*), as absolute immobile power, contains in it the infinite modulations of individual sounds which, led by the idea, gradually arise in it like the waves on the sea's surface when it is moved by the wind. In the second phase, called *paśyantī* (the clear-sighted), there take form on that undiscriminated serene immobility, the images of the archetypes, not yet detached from the background but subtlely disposed there as future propensities. In similar fashion, the indistinct sound, moved by the idea, is stirred up to express itself as though by an interior impulse. The third phase is called *madhyamā* (the intermediate). Here the archetypes are driven towards actuation just as the idea urges the sound to modulate itself in one word or another. In the last phase, *vaikharī*, the archetype is concretely individuated and the sound is expressed in a word suited to the idea. This is the same quarternary scheme reflected in the process from the idea to the Voice, reading from top to bottom. Read the other way round, we have the process of reintegration. The Indian Schools have introduced different variations into these paradigms, with the object of making the same theme accessible through various symbologies, and most especially to aid creatures to find the means most suited to their intelligence and spiritual maturity and most expeditious for inducing the revulsion by meditation upon such paradigms.

The Buddhists of the Great Vehicle translate this same intuition into their own terms, and adapt to it their own system. Of course we should never forget that these ontological constructions are not prompted by speculative curiosity, but by anxiety of a soteriological character. That is to say they define the process of becoming so that it may be overcome. To be eliminated it has to be known. Asaṅga, therefore, admitted three aspects of being: the illusory, that is to say appearance as objectivated in duality (*parikalpita*). As such its manifestations are not existent in themselves, but are conditioned, interdependent and relative (*paratantra*). Both aspects disappear, then, in the absolute moment (*pariniś-panna*) which conditions but also transcends these two limitations, and which is absolute, motionless, impassive power.

But, just as the Yoga Schools add to *suṣupti*, the state of profound sleep, a fourth state, *turīya*, the absolute Being, so the gnostic adepts conceive of a final and more subtle state of Being, beyond the three above-mentioned aspects. For them all these phases are the 'void' but they establish a gradation of the 'void' (*śūnya*), which has obviously several values, because, while all that becomes is void, inasmuch as it is deprived of essence, the supreme void is the Absolute Real inasmuch as it transcends all logical definition.

For these Schools, then, there exist:

(*a*) The Void (*śūnya*), relativity (*paratantra*).
(*b*) The Super-Void (*atiśūnya*), illusory appearance (*parikalpita*).
(*c*) The Great Void (*mahāśūnya, pariniṣpanna*), condition and premise of the two foregoing.
(*d*) The Absolute Void (*sarvaśūnya*), universally luminous consciousness, symbolically Vajradhara.

It is clear that if we read this scheme beginning at the last phase and proceeding to the first we have a process of expansion. The Absolute Void is Absolute Consciousness, non-duality, a coincidence of thought and being, of *nirvāṇa*, and *saṃsāra*, Being in itself of which no predicate is possible. The Great Void is *avidyā* and *māyā*, namely thought in itself, the capacity of all concrete thoughts, the matrix of all the archetypes, which are, however, laid down as a potentiality in it, but are still motionless, indistinct and inseparable from that matrix. This happens through the two poles of illusoriness (*parikalpita*) and relativity (*paratantra*) expressed symbolically in Yoga as day and night. As such, these are susceptible of becoming instruments of salvation because 'that same thought by which fools are bound to *saṃsāra* may become, for ascetics, a means through which they arrive at the condition of Buddha' (*Pañcakrama*, p. 37, v. 11). The

Śākta Schools hold the same view when they say that Mahāmāyā is bivalent because it is *vidyā* and *avidyā* as well: as *vidyā* it is the cause of liberation, as *avidyā* of *saṃsāra*. (*Śāktānanda-taraṅginī*, p. 20)

Other trends interpret these four phases as one diverse intensity of beatitude (*ānanda*) because reintegration is conceived as a union, as a creative act, the journey accomplished by the *ūrdhvaretas*, by him that, as we shall see, restores the seed to its own place in the primordial Male-Female. To these four phases corresponds the arising in the indistinct Absolute of four aspects symbolized in the four bodies of the Buddha, the illusory body (*nirmāṇa*), the paradisal body (*sambhoga*), the body of the *dharma* and the innate body (*sahaja*), to which correspond the four planes of reality, physical, verbal, spiritual and gnostic, *kāya*, *vāk*, *citta* and *jñāna*.

All this process naturally is within us, in a mysterious presence which reveals itself, dazzling in its glory, to the eyes of the initiate. In myself takes place the eternal flux, in me are all the worlds, in me is the mysterious glory of the Buddhas who are disposed in degrees in the spheres of my body which correspond mystically to the various phases of this universal expansion and reabsorption.

Psychical activity, then, hinges upon two correlated but distinct aspects, those of breathing (*prāṇa*) and thinking (*citta*). This supposes a dichotomy of forces which when they act individually continue the work of the psyche, thus that of *karma* and therefore of disintegration. When, on the other hand, movement is arrested in the two lateral canals (*iḍā* and *piṅgalā*) thought is made to flow back into the *caṇḍālī* and this convergence induces the birth of the new man, of the eternal embryo.

A circle is thus completed as in the symbol of the *ouroboros* serpent. From Vajradhara to Vajradhara, from disintegration to reintegration. The Vajradhara principle is illumination (*bodhi*), truth and cognition in one. But it is also the finishing point, after cosmic expansion. This illumination splits into two, that is into *prajñā* and *upāya*, gnosis and means, intuitive element and active element, moon and sun, man and woman, mother and father, as in the symbology of the Buddhist Great Vehicle or of the Śaiva Schools which represent God accompanied by his counterpart, vowel series (*ali*) and consonantal series (*kālī*), female ovum (*rakta*) and seed (*śukla*), by whose conjunction is engendered the egg, the eternal embryo, Vajradhara reborn.

It is a binary division which develops on the opposite sides of the two canals, one to the right and the other to the left, that guide, so to speak, and continue the objectivization of the world of appearances, the splitting of the first principle into duality. This spontaneous scission of the One whereby it appears multiple, as having form whereas it transcends all form, is encouraged and intensified by individual or individualizing thought which, as we saw, borne along by *prāṇa*, develops and intensifies by the play of subjective images the illusion ever renewed. Then the technique of Yoga is used as a help, for it must arrest the individuated or individuating thought. This not only causes the inactivity of *prāṇa* in the two right and left canals, but it also produces a violent reflux of thought—snatched away from its restlessness—towards the *caṇḍālī* where shines the light of the Absolute. The fire which flames in that light burns up thought.

As this process is always ambiguous, the flux of subjective images—which in Śaivism is caused by mental and inborn ignorance—is suppressed. The major co-efficient of duality is arrested. But with this negative phase a positive one is joined. That is to say the re-integration of the Vajrasattva or Vajradhara—the indivisible unity of the Supreme Beatitude (*mahāsukha*)—the return—after the experience of the word displayed in all its multiplicity—to the absolute Identity, which is, indeed, realized when duality has been overcome.

This Unity is Illumination (*bodhicitta*), the *logos spermatikos* which unites indissolubly in itself, gnosis and praxis (*prajñā* and *upāya*) or void (*śūnya*) and compassion (*karuṇā*).

At this point—since, as we know, the universal process is transferred into the microcosm—sexual symbolism is introduced into the system. This *bodhicitta*, the Absolute which must be reintegrated by the conjunction of its two aspects, is the *bindu*, the drop or particle, that is to say the egg created by the mingling of the male seed (*sukla*) and the female ovum (*rakta*), namely *prajñā* and *upāya*, gnosis and praxis, reintegrated, anew, in the primordial Unity.

The symbology which then guides the initiate to the complete realization of his palingenesis becomes very varied and complex. In some Schools the symbology is purely alphabetical, that is to say it is based upon *mantra*, on those formulae which contain in their syllables the mysterious essence of a spiritual plane or of a psychological force. The 'drop' or 'point' (*bindu*), according to this teaching, is the *anusvara*, the sound Ṃ, as in the syllable OṂ. Here the process of cosmic expansion is expressed by the sounds which reproduce, in their various combinations, the intricacy of the divine forces through which the One became multiple. In the instance we are considering, the 'point' is the *anusvara* over the syllable:

$$\text{HŪṂ} = \frac{\text{Ṃ}}{\text{H} + \text{Ū}}$$

that is the consonant (or means) plus the vowel (or gnosis) give the point, the *bodhi*, namely the mystical seed of Vajradhara, the All.

In other Schools, since in the sexual act the egg is formed

by the conjunction of the seed and the ovum, so in the exercise of Yoga from the conjunction of gnosis and means represented by two canals *iḍā* and *piṅgalā*, the egg of reintegration of the primordial Identity is born in the *caṇḍālī* beyond the ephemeral illusion of individual thought.

This egg, indeed, is consciousness which at that very moment flares up in the *caṇḍālī* as a splendid light to dissolve in the upper extremity of the canal—which opens at the summit of the head—in the plane of *nirvāṇa*, beyond the illusory appearance of becoming.

In yet other Schools this conjugation takes place, in reality or allegorically, between the initiate and a woman. The *caṇḍālī*, *mudrā* or *śakti* is almost always a sixteen-year-old girl who, when she is led to the centre of the *maṇḍala*, represents *śakti*, the creative phase, the female aspect of the original Unity. The use of the *mudrā* has become very popular among the Śākta sects and has given rise to a considerable number of errors sharply criticized by the orthodox Schools. There is no doubt that this symbology is very dangerous. It was easy enough to take literally the injunctions of the esoteric liturgy which, to keep initiates at a distance, were not infrequently explained in a deliberately obscene manner.

This happens in some forms of later Buddhism, especially in Bengal (I am alluding to a certain sect called *Sahajīya*), and then also among some Hinduist Schools often influenced by this adulteration which made its appearance in the esoterism of the Diamond Vehicle. All human institutions are subject to corruption and this applies in particular to the Schools which have chosen so audacious a symbolism and which daringly make use of sexual imagery to express their mystical aspirations. But we should not stress these deviations but rather seek to find out what were the ideas of the most authoritative Masters about such delicate matters. Then, also, we should recognize with all frankness, that however dangerous the symbols might be, the techniques of Yoga were very far from taking them literally. The reintegration of Vajradhara is accomplished just as Man is born from the fusion of the ovum and the seed. But even in the case where the liturgical rite accomplished in the *maṇḍala* requires the presence of a woman, the sexual act is not carried to its natural conclusion. The act is controlled by *prāṇa* so that the seed instead of descending goes upwards and rises to the 'lotus of a thousand petals' on the top of the head and there dissolves itself into the uncreated Source of All.

How this is possible is explained both in some of the *Haṭhayoga* treatises and in those of *Sahajīya*. It is a very delicate technique in which use is made, particularly, of breath control. The breath is held in the phase called *kumbhaka*, that is 'retention of breath greatly prolonged'. This blocks the seminal ducts over which the *yogin*'s will acquires as much power as it does on many muscles of the body which, usually, escape our conscious control.

Once again, then, we see that the Masters of the Tantric gnosis keep alive very ancient Indian traditions and are linked with the experiences of that Yoga School which have nourished all the Indian ascetic trends. From the time of the Upanishads, *yogins* have been acquainted with the practices of the *ūrdhvaretas*, of him 'who knows how to lead the semen upwards' (*Maitrī*-Up., 4, 33, *Mahānarayaṇī*-Up., 12, 1).

The Buddhist Masters are very precise on this point: 'Precipitation of the *bodhicitta* (in *Subhaṣita*, p. 77—where *bodhicitta* is taken, as in the esoteric texts, in the sense of 'seed') must not be allowed, because'—they add—'the descent of seed causes the end of passion and the end of passion is the cause of sorrow.' Here, by 'passion' is meant the desire for liberation (*mokṣa*), and 'compassion' because the aim of a Bodhisattva is to lead creatures to the city of *nirvāṇa* by virtue of compassion for him who is ceaselessly thrust by the waves of *saṃsāra* towards an abyss of sorrow. And compassion is indissolubly linked with gnosis.

Compassion and gnosis are the two poles through which develops the process of reintegration or of return which brings to an end the cycle from *bodhicitta*, cause, to *bodhicitta* effect, when phenomenal experience is arrested.

If the neophyte is incapable of being carried back—through this fusion of gnosis and compassion—towards the One, the All, the Absolute, Vajradhara, then the two poles of *bodhicitta* emerge from the cycle and descend on to the objective world into the plane of duality, and this is the falling of the seed.

Naturally, when our body is thought of as a *maṇḍala* there can be no question of the presence of a real, actual *mudrā*, of a sixteen-year-old girl. The *mudrā* in this case is allegorical, and is *caṇḍālī* itself; it is, so to say, the pivot of the Yoga technique, the mysterious canal in which shines the pure light of being.

The idea of an original Unity and of its successive disintegration (from which, all the same, arises the desire to regain the initial state) represents the basis of the religious and mysteriosophical intuition of India. The *Puruṣa* of the Vedas is androgynous.

Likewise Prajāpati (as is told in the *Bṛhadāraṇyaka Upaniṣad*, I, IV, 3), at the beginning of creation, felt alarmed at his own solitude, but then, realizing that there was none other than himself, was convinced that there was no cause to fear anyone. 'He did not feel joy, because no one, when he is alone, feels joy. And he was desirous of another. He was in the same state as are husband and wife in the moment of mutual embrace. So he divided into two and thus husband and wife were produced. However, this was only a part of himself, like a pea divided into two. The void was, in this way, filled by the woman. He approached her. Thus were men born.'

This idea was progressively clarified and expressed in new symbols, but it remained throughout the centuries the keystone of all Indian gnostic thought. We find faint traces of it in the first chapter of the *Guhyasamāja* translated above, when Vajradhara emits from himself a female counterpart. Perhaps the Buddhists, by formulating clearly the thesis of the implicit duality of the thought of Illumination (divided into gnosis and praxis and then reconstituted in the unity of the point (*bindu*)), were the first to define a soteriology in which the male-female binome plays a predominating part. The recondite bivalence of Being is sensed in the depths of the inner experience of each one of us and seen reflected in the play of life as a double polarity between intelligence and psyche, God and nature, being and becoming, and is discussed and defined in complicated systems. It was projected into a liturgy which, as we have seen, is intended to reproduce—by the active participation of man and woman purified by gnosis—the drama of the universe. This separation of Being into gnosis and praxis is repeated, in like manner, in Śivaism, where this same Being is the *śaktimān*, he who possesses in himself *śakti*, the power, the inseparable Unity which, by passing from the state of quietude to activity, becomes infinite plurality.

The same concept is adopted by some Vaishnava sects who seek, in erotic psychology, the reflection of the universal drama. The absolute Principle—so these sects proclaim—is at one and the same time transcendent and immanent. Transcendent as Brahman, immanent as Paramātman, the interior reality of each being. As Bhagavān, that is God, a manifestation in a form accessible to mankind, this principle becomes autocognition and thus the cause of decadence in time and space. This is expressed by the symbol of Krishna, who presents three aspects or powers: essential nature (*svarūpaśakti*), individual power (*jīvaśakti*), by means of which it is multiplied in creatures, magical power (*māyā-*

śakti), by whose operation it evolves in what is other than itself, that is to say in the physical world. Its essential nature is, in its turn, threefold, inasmuch as it summarizes in itself three aspects, which correspond to the classical trinomial of Indian theology: existence (*sat*), consciousness (*cit*), beatitude (*ānanda*). These three aspects are here called 'coexistence' (*samdhinī*), 'consciousness' (*saṃvit*), and 'joy' or 'bliss' (*hladinī*). This blissful power plays a preponderating part in Vaishnava soteriology and underlies that feeling of love (*madhura rasa*) which, exalted and transfigured by religious experience, is the essential attribute of Godhead. It represents the Vaishnava interpretation of the Buddhist *mudrā* or of the *śakti* of the Śaiva sects, the female aspect of God projected into the symbol of Radha and, so sublimated, the instrument of divine achievements. This latter is objective God; God is the subject, and each is stretched towards the other by the impetus of love which restores the original Unity.

When the *Bhāgavatapurāṇa*—and all the literature derived from it—describe, often in a very realistic fashion, the loves of Radha and Krishna in the presence of indulgent female friends (*sakhī*), the Vaishnava devotees read in these pages the drama of the human soul which, when removed from God, alone, is kindled with passion for the divine lover and yearns to become once more united with him in the ecstasies of the of the supreme meeting. The great Vaishnava saints think, like Chaitanya, that they can produce in themselves this state of *Radhābhavā*, the nature of *Radhā*, which consists in the ineffable experience of divine union. For the great number of the devotees there is reserved, however, but the *sakhībhāva*, the state of soul of the female companions, who, according to the legends, facilitate the divine meeting, act as messengers between the two lovers and are witnesses to the beatitude of their meeting. This symbology transports the mystic on to another plane, a supraterrestrial one,

Vṛndāvana, the eternal Vṛndāvana, which is no more the holy earth near Mathurā, but a celestial sphere, beyond the plane of duality. This too is, like the supreme experience of Buddhism and of Śivaism, above the *brahmarandhra*, beyond the *bhūtakoṭi*, the summit of individuated existence; it is the place of identity, in which this world of duality is reabsorbed and transfigured in the plane of erotic Yoga. When the original Man-Woman has been reconstituted the two aspects, consciousness and psyche, the ego and the non-ego, are maintained in a state of unity and poise. On the plane of experience the scission is polarized into two contrasting aspects of Man and Woman. But love, like the *mudrā* of Vajrayāna esoterism, must accomplish the reintegration which is at the same time a sublimation. If the meeting of these two aspects of being should remain limited to the sphere of the senses, there would be—like the fall of *bodhi*—an efflux of seed, a fresh and more grave decadence. Instead of this, no personal satisfaction is sought but a sublimation of spiritual states until the ecstasy of complete spiritual fusion when there is no longer an 'I' and a 'Thou', but only an 'I'. The senses are death, but this transference and sublimation induce the palingenesis, the uncreated, Man, the eternal Man.

'Three sorts of men are known, the inborn eternal man (*sahaja*), the uncreated man, and the body of the *karma* man.'

Such transference is brought about by considering man as enjoyment and woman as beatitude. The relation between the two is not *kāma*, physical love, but *prīti* or *prema* which is the spiritual sublimation of love. This is brought about by substituting (*āropa*) for the psychophysical entity of the ordinary individual, his essential divine nature (*svarūpa*).

'If a man worship this *svarūpa*, then he attains to his human reality. If this substitution does not take place, then a man falls into hell.' (Śivasaṃhitā, 68)

It is the new Man that arises from the old Man, the

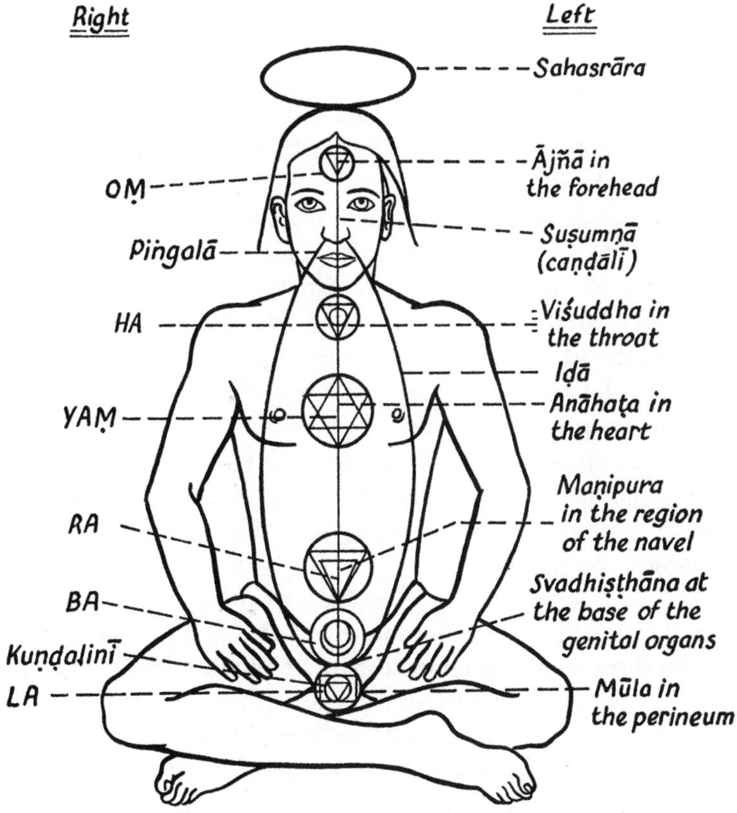

access to the other plane, beyond duality, which is nevertheless realized after a perilous journey on which it is easy to fall into the abyss. Whosoever adventures on this journey without being sufficiently prepared achieves not salvation but perdition.

India is, as it were, overwhelmed with sensuousness. The sun that burns its soil instils fiery ardour into men's blood, a vital impetus that is displayed riotously in the unending exuberance of the jungle, seems to derive substance from the very wasting away of things, and appears to be invigorated by the presence of death which lurks in every place. Opposite Kāli, the terrible Goddess who devours and rends everything, there smiles Durgā, the Great Mother, dispenser of life. Both of these alternate in the world's rhythm as do the steps of dancing Śiva which both create, and destroy, the universe.

In the earliest phase of Indian religious ideas, before the fusion between the indigenous population and the Aryan invaders who invoked, in the Vedic hymns, vague divinities of the sky who dispensed power and earthly prosperity, we find at the Mohendojaro site in the Indus Valley idols and evidence for the early phases of Yoga. Phallic symbols and female images of fecundity appear but also figures of monstrous deities seated in the attitudes of ascetics. On the one hand, the desire to live is expressed in its most crude symbolism, on the other hand, figures which already indicate renunciation abound.

The Upanishad poet, almost overwhelmed with the terrible feeling of the impermanence of all that becomes, and anxious to discover the eternal and immutable Being beyond the flux of forms, opened up a path which was to lead Indian thinkers very far. He denied the world and proclaimed, as did the Buddha, that it was composed of the matter of sorrow. He sought to escape from it into an ineffable peace, leading back into the Brahman, and freeing the luminous purity of the soul from the bonds of the psychophysical complex. He declared that the world and his own psyche were a mirage, an illusory play, a device of God, and that he desired to isolate himself in the motionless, unalterable, colourless light of his divine essence. His own individuality disappeared in that cold gleam, or became submerged in the immensity of God, as a drop of water in the ocean. And so that the world might not distract him, that passions should not disturb him and that from the depths of his soul images should not rise up to affect him, he closed with the aid of

Yoga the gates of the senses, raised himself up to the quietude of contemplation and consecrated his mind on that goal in which he thought, while he was still alive, he would be immersed in the All.

But, in propounding these things, the Indian Masters ran the risk of producing a painful cleavage between the intellect and the psyche, of creating either chilly souls or men immersed in a chaos of primitive intuitions, apprehensive, terrifying, for ever surging up anew from the unexplored depths of the soul. Ascesis on the one hand, superstition on the other, absolute renunciation or formal, outward adaptation to that far-off purification. From this an inevitable flaw is produced in the character, a difficulty in achieving that balance on which life is based. Tantric gnosis, whether Buddhist or Śaiva, attempted to reconstitute the unity which the ascetic ideal had threatened to break: 'In the depths of the body lies a black serpent which gnaws at thee night and day and a man can only with great difficulty free himself of the goad of this *Kāma*.' *Kāma* is not love, but, generically, all instinctive life, the uncontrolled source of procreating and enjoyment.

Indian gnosis took heed of the danger that lies in denying or in extirpating that part of our ego, so the gnostics, instead of following the way of renunciation, turned their attention to transference and the sublimation of the propensity of *kāma* which cannot be suppressed.

Women are not avoided, as they are in the ascetic discipline of the orthodox sects, but become instruments of salvation. Woman is the other part of ourselves and when she is detached from us we feel sorrowful at the loss. She is our completion: psyche and intellect, *yin* and *yang* which anew seek one another so as to re-establish themselves in the primordial equilibrium. Here there is no more any question of the senses. Whoso follows the lure of the senses is *paśu*, the herd, dragged inevitably along the road to annihilation.

But here the person is reborn in a serene harmony where lucid intelligence contemplates and dominates the turbulent riches of the psyche.

The ancient phantasms, the memory of a primitive and far-off world, the monstrous and strange figures of primeval Gods, the fruit of barbarous and cruel intuitions, live on in the depths of our souls and it would be vain to attempt their suppression. They would reappear unexpectedly on the edge of our subconscious. Gnosis does not deny them, does not drive them back, but guides them, as the guests of the senses, towards more noble paths or transforms them.

The images represented in the *maṇḍala,* either as drawn or as imagined in the *maṇḍala* of the human body, retain in many cases their original and fearful aspect, but they are no longer sinister deities of a primitive culture and avid of blood and sacrifices. They have become symbols of phases and forces of the individual and the collective psyche. They are no more projected outside men's souls as implacable and noxious powers, but they are cognized as facts of experience. They do not, then, rise up any more as threatening phantasms that disintegrate and corrupt the personality, but they are docile and obey the commands of the mystic in a state of appeasement and serenity on which shines the light of consciousness regained.

When, then, the Indian or Tibetan artist designs a *maṇḍala* he is not obeying the arbitrary command of caprice. He is following a definite tradition which teaches him how to represent, in a particular manner, the very drama of his soul. He does not depict on a *maṇḍala* the cold images of an iconographical text, but he pours out upon it the phantasms of his subconscious ego and thus knows them and liberates himself from them. He gives form to that world he feels surging within him and he sees it spread out before his eyes, no longer the invisible and unrestrainable master of his soul, but a serene symbolic representation which reveals to him the secrets of things and of himself. This complicated juxtaposition of images, their symmetrical arrangement, this alternation of calm and of menacing figures, is the open book of the world and of Man's own spirit.

Where once there was darkness now there is light.

APPENDIX OF ILLUSTRATIONS WITH EXPLANATIONS

PLATE I

Maṇḍala of rDorjeac'aṅ, the Holder of the Diamond, that is of consciousness as pure, luminous and indefectible as a diamond, synthesis of all the Buddhas, because they are fundamentally this same luminosity, or, as the Śaivas would say, 'thought glittering through its essence' (*prabhāsvara citta*)—this Absolute Consciousness (parāsaṃvit).

The inside square comprises the essential and most secret part of the *maṇḍala*. In this figure are displayed, as leaves of the mystical lotus, the five families, the initial phase of cosmic dichotomy. In some *maṇḍalas* their place is taken by two triangles called 'The Wellspring of *Dharma*' (*c'os hbyuṅ, dharmodaya*). The *Dharma* is naturally understood as the Absolute Real and, at the same time as its revelation, the Word identified with the Buddha and with the person of the mystic who, by liturgical acts and the revulsion of planes, has projected himself into that ideal centre from which everything emanates, to which everything returns and around which everything develops.

'The Wellspring of the Law' is represented by two intersecting triangles which indicate the way of expansion from the One to the All (apex downwards) and of return or reintegration (apex upwards). In the symbology of the Śaiva or Śākta sects the two triangles represent the power (*śakti*) and Śiva. In the centre of the lotus (which is circumscribed by the intersecting triangles) is the Twofold Diamond (*vajra, adamas*) that indicates the indefectible plane, the Immutable Absolute, the Supreme Consciousness. This *maṇḍala* is divided into two *maṇḍala* cities, the one inside and the other outside, separated from one another by an intermediate space in which are placed adoring deities, symbols of the light imprisoned in the psyche, and which awakens the primordial consciousness.

The five strips which delimit this inside square define the *templum*, the sacred city, the projection of the other plane which circumscribes and encloses the *mysterium magnum*.

The four gates or points of access to the above-mentioned plane are surmounted by complex superstructures modelled on the doors of royal palaces and open on to the four sides.

In the space between the above-mentioned square and the first inside circle are to be seen various ornaments—umbrellas, vases, standards—symbols of the utensils used in the rituals, offerings designed to honour sacred places and a sign of the divine surfaces, the territory of the *sacer*, the residence of the King.

The first inside circle is composed of a ring of lotus leaves turned outwards to indicate the mystic's accessibility to the secret. Then comes the diamond girdle, the boundary between the world of becoming—the descent—and the initial phase of the return, or reintegration. Outside is the circle of fire, gnosis that destroys ignorance.

PLATE II

Maṇḍala of Saṃvara in the Temple of the *Maṇḍalas* at Toling, Western Tibet. The Temple of the *Maṇḍalas* with three planes was reserved for initiations and the bestowing of baptisms when the neophytes were put by the Masters before the *maṇḍalas* composed of the different esoteric cycles into which they were to be initiated.

In the centre is represented the God coupled with his counterpart and, on the four sides, the other four deities who make up the pentad, the first scission. Between each figure and the next, and at the intermediate points, are four cups made from skulls. They are filled with blood, as symbols of the supreme beatitude which is experienced when return takes place, that is when the efflux of the creative powers, the disintegration in the world of nature and of the psyche, is arrested and consciousness has recovered its primordial unity. In the three concentric circles which follow are placed deities who represent $8 + 8 + 8 = 24$ heroes, the emanations of the God which protect his infinite expansion, the mysterious presence of consciousness on every plane of being. In the four corners and at the four gates are the eight protectors of the cardinal points, the defenders of consciousness from all possible disintegration. On the outer edge are the sixteen sciences, the multiform eternal adoration, the beatitude that is the mark of liberty reconquered.

PLATE III

This *maṇḍala*—which displays, in graphic synthesis, the abstruse mysteriosophical theories of the Śākta School—is drawn up according to a scheme which the *Saundarya-laharī* (a very celebrated poem of Indian esoterism, written, according to tradition, by one of the most profound of Indian thinkers) describes in a way that is deliberately enigmatic:

'The corners which make up Thy dwelling are divided into forty-four, that is the nine fundamental natures, that is to say, the four Śrīkantha and the five damsels of Śiva, all detached from Śambu, together with the eight-petalled lotus, the sixteen-petalled lotus, the three circles and the three lines' (XI). The 'nine fundamental natures' correspond to the basic triangles drawn parallel to the diameter of the *maṇḍala.* These serve to indicate the pattern into which duality evolves from unity, the process and the mode of differentiation. Consequently these are called the 'nine wombs' and correspond to the nine elements of which the microcosm is made up, that is to say the 'five damsels' of Śiva: skin, blood, flesh, fat, bones—emanations of the Śakti; the 'four Śrīkantha' (Śrīkantha is an epithet of Śiva): marrow, seed, vital energy and individual soul (jīva) in the macrocosm emanated by Śiva. In similar fashion the five material elements: earth (solidity), water (fluidity), fire (heat), air (motion) and ether (space); the five subtle elements: smell (earth in its subtle state), taste (water in its subtle state), form (fire in its subtle state), touch (air in its subtle state), sound (ether); the five organs of perception: hearing, touch, sight, taste, smelling; the five organs of action: speech, hands and feet, organs of evacuation, organs of generation and mind which summarizes or reacts to the impressions of the senses. All this is descended from Śiva (śuddhavidyā). Then come *Māyā,* unlimited creative energy (which, by operating in Śiva, is responsible for the idea that what exists is different from him); then pure knowledge, by which Śiva identifies himself with what exists and thinks: 'I am This'; then Maheśvara, the Universal Being, and finally Sadāśiva, the Being collected in himself; these are the four successive manifestations of Śiva declined from his primordial brilliancy.

Therefore, in these nine triangles is expressed the process of divine expansion, which proceeds from the One to the Many, to Macrocosm and Microcosm and is the eclipse of the non-Ego. Śambu, in the centre, is the potential point, the origin of everything. The three lines enclose the two rows of lotus leaves respectively with eight petals in the outer circuit and sixteen petals in the inner circuit. The significance of the lotus has already been mentioned. The letters of the alphabet, placed on the different petals and at the corners, correspond to various Powers and each one is marked with the name of a Goddess. Thus is obtained a visible, though symbolical, expression of the continuous efflux and return of consciousness which manifest and dissolve the psychophysical complex. This *maṇḍala*, therefore, is considered as the exterior sacrifice inasmuch as it needs lines and letters in a visible pattern, but upon it is superposed, in a second phase, the interior sacrifice, the transposition of the *maṇḍala* into the body of the initiate, identified mystically with Śiva, the Supreme Consciousness, which is mysteriously present within him.

'Thou in the lotus of a thousand petals then uniteth thyself with thy Lord after having purified all the way of the family of the Powers, the earth in the fundamental base (Mūlādhāra), the water in the jewel-decked city (Maṇipura), the fire in its own dwelling (Svādiṣṭhāna), the air of the heart (Anāhata), the ether above (in the wheel of purity, Viśuddhi) and the mind (in the wheel of command (Ājñā), between the two eyes). (IX)

'After having infused in the cosmic expansion the currents of ambrosia emanating from thy feet, thou (descending) from the resplendent lunar mansions (that is objective consciousness) reassume thy original position in the Mūlādhāra and having taken on the aspect of a serpent lying in three and a half coils asleep in the cavity of the orifice of Kulakuṇḍa' (X). These two lines of verse describe what Indian mystics call the 'ladder' or 'stairs' of the secret of Kuṇḍalinī, the pure consciousness hidden within us which in the macrocosm is termed *Tripurasundarī*, 'the beauty of the three cities', and in the microcosm *kuṇḍalinī*. The Yogin, by his art of breath-control and by mystical cognition, induces its awakening and its progressive ascent through the 'wheels' or psychic centres. These psychic centres, penetrated by its luminosity, dissolve and with them (on the parallel plane of the macrocosm) there are eliminated the five elements of which things are composed. In our persons there is, by the substitution of psychic symbology for the material equivalence, a progressive ascent from the confused and dark to the pure and clear, until *kuṇḍalinī*, after overcoming the five wheels (that is, as the poem says, the collection of Powers), rises up to the *Śrīcakra* or the lotus of a thousand petals in which this divine Power, by virtue of which Śiva creates and is multiplied in the All, is reunited in the beatitude of the primordial communion with Śiva. At this moment the meditator dissolves his own psyche and reposes in the beatitude of *nirvāṇa*, *nirvāṇa* in this life which lasts as long as he manages to maintain *kuṇḍalinī* thus reunited with Śiva. Since this state of reintegration cannot last for ever, as soon as he emerges from it the descending process begins, the fall in time and space, the splitting into the psychophysical complex, the transmutation into materiality. Then *kuṇḍalinī* permeates the wheels and these begin to form. Therefore in the verse quoted above it is said that *kuṇḍalinī* infuses ambrosia into the cosmic expansion, that is into the collection of Powers which are identified with the body correlated with the macrocosm. The many millions of canals which nourish its life are, in macrocosmic correspondence, the equivalent of the display of the universe, of the All. When the descent has been accomplished, and therefore the creative process reproduced, *kuṇḍalinī* reaches the lowest wheel and stays there, coiled up, and asleep in the pericarp of the four-petalled lotus in the middle of that wheel. Thus the macrocosm and the microcosm have appeared once more.

With this repeated exercise, described and directed in its various phases by Yoga, the meditator is able to unite himself with the Power that moves all things, from which everything arises and to which all returns.

'When one desires to praise thee with the words "O Bhavāni, mayest thou cast a look of pity upon thy servant" (or "may I be in thee"), at that moment thou grantest to him identity with thyself, a state that is brilliant by the light reflected from the diadems of the Gods who bow before him, as they do before Thee' (XXII). Thus is attained the Absolute Identity, that is the Power, the Supreme Consciousness which transcends all possible divine manifestations. Nor is all this illusory, since all to which the human psyche gives life, the ideas in which men believe (and which therefore often remain active and fruitful on earth and as the cause of good and evil accomplished or suffered) are true and real.

'But they are not eternal forms, in the sense that the Supreme Power surpasses them all and since from it they derive their origin and their form, only cognition of this Supreme Reality eliminates and surpasses all. This mysterious sacrifice of *kuṇḍalinī* which reproduces, by the conscious will of the initiate, the eternal play of forces which the free necessity of God urges to produce the multiplicity of things and of creatures, time and space, ideas and imaginations—draws the initiate away from the disintegration of life, aids him to rise up from the abyss into which *māyā* has plunged him and to find in the light of the Power, his mysterious Ego. As the poets of the Upanishads say "*Tat tvam asi*"—"Thou art that one." Or rather as the Śaiva Masters declare: "In the sight of this Supreme God that is pure Illumination, *ātmā*, what need is there of means (to reach him)?" It is not the attainment of his essence since that is always eternal in each one of us. Nor is it cognition since this is of itself illuminating; there are no obstacles to be removed, because there are none there, neither is it possible to enter into him since there is no one who can do so as distinct from him. What means can there be then, since it is logically impossible to admit that such means exist separate from him? Since all the universe is one reality which is only consciousness, which is not divided by time, neither delimited by space, nor imprisoned by limits, which is circumscribed by no form, is not explainable in words, and not declared by any knowledge, but which assumes by its own will its own attributes as set out above. And this reality is autonomous cognition, I am it (the real) and in it (that is) in myself all is reflected. For this reason whoever thus firmly discriminates is at once immersed for ever

PLATE I The Maṇḍala of rDorjeac'aṅ, the Holder of the Diamond

PLATE II The Maṇḍala of Saṃvara

PLATE III The Maṇḍala of the Śrīcakra

PLATE IV A Chinese mirror

in the divine Consciousness and no longer needs ritual formulae, offerings, meditation, liturgies and other similar prescriptions.' (From the Tantrasāra of Abhinavagupta)

PLATE IV

Some Chinese mirrors are known, because of certain designs with which they are ornamented and which suggest the capital letters T.L.V., as 'T.L.V. mirrors'. These have been considered as sundials, which they are not. They are *maṇḍala* schemes of the universe—round heaven, the pole star or *axis mundi* in the middle; square earth; the four gates of the Chung-kuo of China or of the royal palace correlated with the *axis mundi*. The graphic representation of schemes of the universe which are made in this manner serve, none the less, a magic end, that of Return, of Unification with the central point from which, as soon as it has been attained, is derived the omnipotence of him who has achieved this. The *Tao*—first principle and Prime Mover of all things (see *Karlgren*: Early Chinese Mirror Inscriptions, p. 31, in the *Bulletin of the Museum of Far Eastern Antiquities*, No. 6 (Stockholm, 1934))—is identified with the centre and unity: 'May your eight sons and nine grandsons,' reads the inscription on one of these mirrors, 'govern the centre'; that is, may they unite themselves with the Supreme Mover, source of immortality and of thaumaturgical power. The grandsons are nine because nine is the perfect number; specifically, four females, even number, *Yin*, the female principle, the moon; and five males, odd number, *Yang*, the male principle, the sun (cf Karlgren, p. 43). Elsewhere, ibid., p. 29: 'If you ascend the (mountain) T'ai-shan, you will see the divine men; they eat the essence of jade and drink the limpid spring; they have attained to the Way of Heaven; all things are in their natural state; they yoke the Hornless Dragon to their chariot; they mount the floating clouds; may you have office and rank, may you preserve your sons and grandsons.'

INDEX

A

Abhiṣeka ('coronation'), 44
Activity, psychic, 120
Adhiṣṭhāna, 88
Antarjyotir-māyā ('interior light'), 5
Archetypes in the soul of Man, ix
Ātmā ('pure illumination') 140
Ātman ('secret self'), 2, 5, 10, 11, 28
Autoconsciousness, 2
Avalokiteśvara, evocation of, 90, 95
Axis mundi, 25

B

Baptism, 44, 105
Bardo (period immediately after death), 6–8, 26
Being, five modes of in Śaiva Schools, 55
Being, four aspects of among the Gnostics, 119
Being, the Absolute, 55
Being, three aspects of in Great Vehicle Buddhism, 118
Bindu, 47
Bodhgaya, 86
Bodhi necessary for reintegration 58, 109
Bodhicitta (human consciousness), 15
Bodhimaṇḍala (ideal centre of the world), 19
Bodhisattva, role of, 19, 57, 58, 112, 124
Body as a support, 111
Bon Po, indigenous religion of Tibet, 24
Brahma, the essence of, 65
Brahman, 130
Brahmarandhra, 87, 108, 117
Buddha, consubstantiation with, 65–67
Buddhi, definition of, 11
Buddhism, Diamond Vehicle, 50
Buddhism, Great Vehicle, 5, 15, 118
Buddhism, pantheon in, 74
Buddhism, primitive, 2, 5

C

Cakravartin (the Universal Monarch), 23, 43, 44
Canals in the body, 113
Caṇḍālī, 113, 114
Categories, psychological, 78

L

M

N

O

P

A CATALOG OF SELECTED DOVER BOOKS IN ALL FIELDS OF INTEREST

CONCERNING THE SPIRITUAL IN ART, Wassily Kandinsky. Pioneering work by father of abstract art. Thoughts on color theory, nature of art. Analysis of earlier masters. 12 illustrations. 80pp. of text. 5⅜ x 8½. 23411-8

ANIMALS: 1,419 Copyright-Free Illustrations of Mammals, Birds, Fish, Insects, etc., Jim Harter (ed.). Clear wood engravings present, in extremely lifelike poses, over 1,000 species of animals. One of the most extensive pictorial sourcebooks of its kind. Captions. Index. 284pp. 9 x 12. 23766-4

CELTIC ART: The Methods of Construction, George Bain. Simple geometric techniques for making Celtic interlacements, spirals, Kells-type initials, animals, humans, etc. Over 500 illustrations. 160pp. 9 x 12. (Available in U.S. only.) 22923-8

AN ATLAS OF ANATOMY FOR ARTISTS, Fritz Schider. Most thorough reference work on art anatomy in the world. Hundreds of illustrations, including selections from works by Vesalius, Leonardo, Goya, Ingres, Michelangelo, others. 593 illustrations. 192pp. 7⅛ x 10¼. 20241-0

CELTIC HAND STROKE-BY-STROKE (Irish Half-Uncial from "The Book of Kells"): An Arthur Baker Calligraphy Manual, Arthur Baker. Complete guide to creating each letter of the alphabet in distinctive Celtic manner. Covers hand position, strokes, pens, inks, paper, more. Illustrated. 48pp. 8¼ x 11. 24336-2

EASY ORIGAMI, John Montroll. Charming collection of 32 projects (hat, cup, pelican, piano, swan, many more) specially designed for the novice origami hobbyist. Clearly illustrated easy-to-follow instructions insure that even beginning papercrafters will achieve successful results. 48pp. 8¼ x 11. 27298-2

THE COMPLETE BOOK OF BIRDHOUSE CONSTRUCTION FOR WOODWORKERS, Scott D. Campbell. Detailed instructions, illustrations, tables. Also data on bird habitat and instinct patterns. Bibliography. 3 tables. 63 illustrations in 15 figures. 48pp. 5¼ x 8½. 24407-5

BLOOMINGDALE'S ILLUSTRATED 1886 CATALOG: Fashions, Dry Goods and Housewares, Bloomingdale Brothers. Famed merchants' extremely rare catalog depicting about 1,700 products: clothing, housewares, firearms, dry goods, jewelry, more. Invaluable for dating, identifying vintage items. Also, copyright-free graphics for artists, designers. Co-published with Henry Ford Museum & Greenfield Village. 160pp. 8¼ x 11. 25780-0

HISTORIC COSTUME IN PICTURES, Braun & Schneider. Over 1,450 costumed figures in clearly detailed engravings–from dawn of civilization to end of 19th century. Captions. Many folk costumes. 256pp. 8⅝ x 11¾. 23150-X

THE CLARINET AND CLARINET PLAYING, David Pino. Lively, comprehensive work features suggestions about technique, musicianship, and musical interpretation, as well as guidelines for teaching, making your own reeds, and preparing for public performance. Includes an intriguing look at clarinet history. "A godsend," *The Clarinet,* Journal of the International Clarinet Society. Appendixes. 7 illus. 320pp. 5⅜ x 8½. 40270-3

HOLLYWOOD GLAMOR PORTRAITS, John Kobal (ed.). 145 photos from 1926-49. Harlow, Gable, Bogart, Bacall; 94 stars in all. Full background on photographers, technical aspects. 160pp. 8⅜ x 11¼. 23352-9

THE ANNOTATED CASEY AT THE BAT: A Collection of Ballads about the Mighty Casey/Third, Revised Edition, Martin Gardner (ed.). Amusing sequels and parodies of one of America's best-loved poems: Casey's Revenge, Why Casey Whiffed, Casey's Sister at the Bat, others. 256pp. 5⅜ x 8½. 28598-7

THE RAVEN AND OTHER FAVORITE POEMS, Edgar Allan Poe. Over 40 of the author's most memorable poems: "The Bells," "Ulalume," "Israfel," "To Helen," "The Conqueror Worm," "Eldorado," "Annabel Lee," many more. Alphabetic lists of titles and first lines. 64pp. 5$\frac{3}{16}$ x 8¼. 26685-0

PERSONAL MEMOIRS OF U. S. GRANT, Ulysses Simpson Grant. Intelligent, deeply moving firsthand account of Civil War campaigns, considered by many the finest military memoirs ever written. Includes letters, historic photographs, maps and more. 528pp. 6⅛ x 9¼. 28587-1

ANCIENT EGYPTIAN MATERIALS AND INDUSTRIES, A. Lucas and J. Harris. Fascinating, comprehensive, thoroughly documented text describes this ancient civilization's vast resources and the processes that incorporated them in daily life, including the use of animal products, building materials, cosmetics, perfumes and incense, fibers, glazed ware, glass and its manufacture, materials used in the mummification process, and much more. 544pp. 6⅛ x 9¼. (Available in U.S. only.) 40446-3

RUSSIAN STORIES/RUSSKIE RASSKAZY: A Dual-Language Book, edited by Gleb Struve. Twelve tales by such masters as Chekhov, Tolstoy, Dostoevsky, Pushkin, others. Excellent word-for-word English translations on facing pages, plus teaching and study aids, Russian/English vocabulary, biographical/critical introductions, more. 416pp. 5⅜ x 8½. 26244-8

PHILADELPHIA THEN AND NOW: 60 Sites Photographed in the Past and Present, Kenneth Finkel and Susan Oyama. Rare photographs of City Hall, Logan Square, Independence Hall, Betsy Ross House, other landmarks juxtaposed with contemporary views. Captures changing face of historic city. Introduction. Captions. 128pp. 8¼ x 11. 25790-8

AIA ARCHITECTURAL GUIDE TO NASSAU AND SUFFOLK COUNTIES, LONG ISLAND, The American Institute of Architects, Long Island Chapter, and the Society for the Preservation of Long Island Antiquities. Comprehensive, well-researched and generously illustrated volume brings to life over three centuries of Long Island's great architectural heritage. More than 240 photographs with authoritative, extensively detailed captions. 176pp. 8¼ x 11. 26946-9

NORTH AMERICAN INDIAN LIFE: Customs and Traditions of 23 Tribes, Elsie Clews Parsons (ed.). 27 fictionalized essays by noted anthropologists examine religion, customs, government, additional facets of life among the Winnebago, Crow, Zuni, Eskimo, other tribes. 480pp. 6⅛ x 9¼. 27377-6

FRANK LLOYD WRIGHT'S DANA HOUSE, Donald Hoffmann. Pictorial essay of residential masterpiece with over 160 interior and exterior photos, plans, elevations, sketches and studies. 128pp. $9\frac{1}{4} \times 10\frac{3}{4}$. 29120-0

THE MALE AND FEMALE FIGURE IN MOTION: 60 Classic Photographic Sequences, Eadweard Muybridge. 60 true-action photographs of men and women walking, running, climbing, bending, turning, etc., reproduced from rare 19th-century masterpiece. vi + 121pp. 9 x 12. 24745-7

1001 QUESTIONS ANSWERED ABOUT THE SEASHORE, N. J. Berrill and Jacquelyn Berrill. Queries answered about dolphins, sea snails, sponges, starfish, fishes, shore birds, many others. Covers appearance, breeding, growth, feeding, much more. 305pp. $5\frac{1}{4} \times 8\frac{1}{4}$. 23366-9

ATTRACTING BIRDS TO YOUR YARD, William J. Weber. Easy-to-follow guide offers advice on how to attract the greatest diversity of birds: birdhouses, feeders, water and waterers, much more. 96pp. $5\frac{3}{16} \times 8\frac{1}{4}$. 28927-3

MEDICINAL AND OTHER USES OF NORTH AMERICAN PLANTS: A Historical Survey with Special Reference to the Eastern Indian Tribes, Charlotte Erichsen-Brown. Chronological historical citations document 500 years of usage of plants, trees, shrubs native to eastern Canada, northeastern U.S. Also complete identifying information. 343 illustrations. 544pp. $6\frac{1}{2} \times 9\frac{1}{4}$. 25951-X

STORYBOOK MAZES, Dave Phillips. 23 stories and mazes on two-page spreads: Wizard of Oz, Treasure Island, Robin Hood, etc. Solutions. 64pp. $8\frac{1}{4} \times 11$. 23628-5

AMERICAN NEGRO SONGS: 230 Folk Songs and Spirituals, Religious and Secular, John W. Work. This authoritative study traces the African influences of songs sung and played by black Americans at work, in church, and as entertainment. The author discusses the lyric significance of such songs as "Swing Low, Sweet Chariot," "John Henry," and others and offers the words and music for 230 songs. Bibliography. Index of Song Titles. 272pp. $6\frac{1}{2} \times 9\frac{1}{4}$. 40271-1

MOVIE-STAR PORTRAITS OF THE FORTIES, John Kobal (ed.). 163 glamor, studio photos of 106 stars of the 1940s: Rita Hayworth, Ava Gardner, Marlon Brando, Clark Gable, many more. 176pp. $8\frac{3}{8} \times 11\frac{1}{4}$. 23546-7

BENCHLEY LOST AND FOUND, Robert Benchley. Finest humor from early 30s, about pet peeves, child psychologists, post office and others. Mostly unavailable elsewhere. 73 illustrations by Peter Arno and others. 183pp. $5\frac{3}{8} \times 8\frac{1}{2}$. 22410-4

YEKL and THE IMPORTED BRIDEGROOM AND OTHER STORIES OF YIDDISH NEW YORK, Abraham Cahan. Film Hester Street based on *Yekl* (1896). Novel, other stories among first about Jewish immigrants on N.Y.'s East Side. 240pp. $5\frac{3}{8} \times 8\frac{1}{2}$. 22427-9

SELECTED POEMS, Walt Whitman. Generous sampling from *Leaves of Grass*. Twenty-four poems include "I Hear America Singing," "Song of the Open Road," "I Sing the Body Electric," "When Lilacs Last in the Dooryard Bloom'd," "O Captain! My Captain!"–all reprinted from an authoritative edition. Lists of titles and first lines. 128pp. $5\frac{3}{16} \times 8\frac{1}{4}$. 26878-0

THE BEST TALES OF HOFFMANN, E. T. A. Hoffmann. 10 of Hoffmann's most important stories: "Nutcracker and the King of Mice," "The Golden Flowerpot," etc. 458pp. 5⅜ x 8½. 21793-0

FROM FETISH TO GOD IN ANCIENT EGYPT, E. A. Wallis Budge. Rich detailed survey of Egyptian conception of "God" and gods, magic, cult of animals, Osiris, more. Also, superb English translations of hymns and legends. 240 illustrations. 545pp. 5⅜ x 8½. 25803-3

FRENCH STORIES/CONTES FRANÇAIS: A Dual-Language Book, Wallace Fowlie. Ten stories by French masters, Voltaire to Camus: "Micromegas" by Voltaire; "The Atheist's Mass" by Balzac; "Minuet" by de Maupassant; "The Guest" by Camus, six more. Excellent English translations on facing pages. Also French-English vocabulary list, exercises, more. 352pp. 5⅜ x 8½. 26443-2

CHICAGO AT THE TURN OF THE CENTURY IN PHOTOGRAPHS: 122 Historic Views from the Collections of the Chicago Historical Society, Larry A. Viskochil. Rare large-format prints offer detailed views of City Hall, State Street, the Loop, Hull House, Union Station, many other landmarks, circa 1904-1913. Introduction. Captions. Maps. 144pp. 9⅜ x 12¼. 24656-6

OLD BROOKLYN IN EARLY PHOTOGRAPHS, 1865-1929, William Lee Younger. Luna Park, Gravesend race track, construction of Grand Army Plaza, moving of Hotel Brighton, etc. 157 previously unpublished photographs. 165pp. 8⅞ x 11¾. 23587-4

THE MYTHS OF THE NORTH AMERICAN INDIANS, Lewis Spence. Rich anthology of the myths and legends of the Algonquins, Iroquois, Pawnees and Sioux, prefaced by an extensive historical and ethnological commentary. 36 illustrations. 480pp. 5⅜ x 8½. 25967-6

AN ENCYCLOPEDIA OF BATTLES: Accounts of Over 1,560 Battles from 1479 B.C. to the Present, David Eggenberger. Essential details of every major battle in recorded history from the first battle of Megiddo in 1479 B.C. to Grenada in 1984. List of Battle Maps. New Appendix covering the years 1967-1984. Index. 99 illustrations. 544pp. 6½ x 9¼. 24913-1

SAILING ALONE AROUND THE WORLD, Captain Joshua Slocum. First man to sail around the world, alone, in small boat. One of great feats of seamanship told in delightful manner. 67 illustrations. 294pp. 5⅜ x 8½. 20326-3

ANARCHISM AND OTHER ESSAYS, Emma Goldman. Powerful, penetrating, prophetic essays on direct action, role of minorities, prison reform, puritan hypocrisy, violence, etc. 271pp. 5⅜ x 8½. 22484-8

MYTHS OF THE HINDUS AND BUDDHISTS, Ananda K. Coomaraswamy and Sister Nivedita. Great stories of the epics; deeds of Krishna, Shiva, taken from puranas, Vedas, folk tales; etc. 32 illustrations. 400pp. 5⅜ x 8½. 21759-0

THE TRAUMA OF BIRTH, Otto Rank. Rank's controversial thesis that anxiety neurosis is caused by profound psychological trauma which occurs at birth. 256pp. 5⅜ x 8½. 27974-X

A THEOLOGICO-POLITICAL TREATISE, Benedict Spinoza. Also contains unfinished Political Treatise. Great classic on religious liberty, theory of government on common consent. R. Elwes translation. Total of 421pp. 5⅜ x 8½. 20249-6

MY BONDAGE AND MY FREEDOM, Frederick Douglass. Born a slave, Douglass became outspoken force in antislavery movement. The best of Douglass' autobiographies. Graphic description of slave life. 464pp. 5⅜ x 8½. 22457-0

FOLLOWING THE EQUATOR: A Journey Around the World, Mark Twain. Fascinating humorous account of 1897 voyage to Hawaii, Australia, India, New Zealand, etc. Ironic, bemused reports on peoples, customs, climate, flora and fauna, politics, much more. 197 illustrations. 720pp. 5⅜ x 8½. 26113-1

THE PEOPLE CALLED SHAKERS, Edward D. Andrews. Definitive study of Shakers: origins, beliefs, practices, dances, social organization, furniture and crafts, etc. 33 illustrations. 351pp. 5⅜ x 8½. 21081-2

THE MYTHS OF GREECE AND ROME, H. A. Guerber. A classic of mythology, generously illustrated, long prized for its simple, graphic, accurate retelling of the principal myths of Greece and Rome, and for its commentary on their origins and significance. With 64 illustrations by Michelangelo, Raphael, Titian, Rubens, Canova, Bernini and others. 480pp. 5⅜ x 8½. 27584-1

PSYCHOLOGY OF MUSIC, Carl E. Seashore. Classic work discusses music as a medium from psychological viewpoint. Clear treatment of physical acoustics, auditory apparatus, sound perception, development of musical skills, nature of musical feeling, host of other topics. 88 figures. 408pp. 5⅜ x 8½. 21851-1

THE PHILOSOPHY OF HISTORY, Georg W. Hegel. Great classic of Western thought develops concept that history is not chance but rational process, the evolution of freedom. 457pp. 5⅜ x 8½. 20112-0

THE BOOK OF TEA, Kakuzo Okakura. Minor classic of the Orient: entertaining, charming explanation, interpretation of traditional Japanese culture in terms of tea ceremony. 94pp. 5⅜ x 8½. 20070-1

LIFE IN ANCIENT EGYPT, Adolf Erman. Fullest, most thorough, detailed older account with much not in more recent books, domestic life, religion, magic, medicine, commerce, much more. Many illustrations reproduce tomb paintings, carvings, hieroglyphs, etc. 597pp. 5⅜ x 8½. 22632-8

SUNDIALS, Their Theory and Construction, Albert Waugh. Far and away the best, most thorough coverage of ideas, mathematics concerned, types, construction, adjusting anywhere. Simple, nontechnical treatment allows even children to build several of these dials. Over 100 illustrations. 230pp. 5⅜ x 8½. 22947-5

THEORETICAL HYDRODYNAMICS, L. M. Milne-Thomson. Classic exposition of the mathematical theory of fluid motion, applicable to both hydrodynamics and aerodynamics. Over 600 exercises. 768pp. 6⅛ x 9¼. 68970-0

SONGS OF EXPERIENCE: Facsimile Reproduction with 26 Plates in Full Color, William Blake. 26 full-color plates from a rare 1826 edition. Includes "The Tyger," "London," "Holy Thursday," and other poems. Printed text of poems. 48pp. 5¼ x 7. 24636-1

OLD-TIME VIGNETTES IN FULL COLOR, Carol Belanger Grafton (ed.). Over 390 charming, often sentimental illustrations, selected from archives of Victorian graphics–pretty women posing, children playing, food, flowers, kittens and puppies, smiling cherubs, birds and butterflies, much more. All copyright-free. 48pp. 9¼ x 12¼. 27269-9

LITTLE BOOK OF EARLY AMERICAN CRAFTS AND TRADES, Peter Stockham (ed.). 1807 children's book explains crafts and trades: baker, hatter, cooper, potter, and many others. 23 copperplate illustrations. 140pp. 4⅝ x 6. 23336-7

VICTORIAN FASHIONS AND COSTUMES FROM HARPER'S BAZAR, 1867–1898, Stella Blum (ed.). Day costumes, evening wear, sports clothes, shoes, hats, other accessories in over 1,000 detailed engravings. 320pp. 9⅜ x 12¼. 22990-4

GUSTAV STICKLEY, THE CRAFTSMAN, Mary Ann Smith. Superb study surveys broad scope of Stickley's achievement, especially in architecture. Design philosophy, rise and fall of the Craftsman empire, descriptions and floor plans for many Craftsman houses, more. 86 black-and-white halftones. 31 line illustrations. Introduction 208pp. 6½ x 9¼. 27210-9

THE LONG ISLAND RAIL ROAD IN EARLY PHOTOGRAPHS, Ron Ziel. Over 220 rare photos, informative text document origin (1844) and development of rail service on Long Island. Vintage views of early trains, locomotives, stations, passengers, crews, much more. Captions. 8⅞ x 11¾. 26301-0

VOYAGE OF THE LIBERDADE, Joshua Slocum. Great 19th-century mariner's thrilling, first-hand account of the wreck of his ship off South America, the 35-foot boat he built from the wreckage, and its remarkable voyage home. 128pp. 5⅜ x 8½. 40022-0

TEN BOOKS ON ARCHITECTURE, Vitruvius. The most important book ever written on architecture. Early Roman aesthetics, technology, classical orders, site selection, all other aspects. Morgan translation. 331pp. 5⅜ x 8½. 20645-9

THE HUMAN FIGURE IN MOTION, Eadweard Muybridge. More than 4,500 stopped-action photos, in action series, showing undraped men, women, children jumping, lying down, throwing, sitting, wrestling, carrying, etc. 390pp. 7⅞ x 10⅝. 20204-6 Clothbd.

TREES OF THE EASTERN AND CENTRAL UNITED STATES AND CANADA, William M. Harlow. Best one-volume guide to 140 trees. Full descriptions, woodlore, range, etc. Over 600 illustrations. Handy size. 288pp. 4½ x 6⅜. 20395-6

SONGS OF WESTERN BIRDS, Dr. Donald J. Borror. Complete song and call repertoire of 60 western species, including flycatchers, juncoes, cactus wrens, many more–includes fully illustrated booklet. Cassette and manual 99913-0

GROWING AND USING HERBS AND SPICES, Milo Miloradovich. Versatile handbook provides all the information needed for cultivation and use of all the herbs and spices available in North America. 4 illustrations. Index. Glossary. 236pp. 5⅜ x 8½. 25058-X

BIG BOOK OF MAZES AND LABYRINTHS, Walter Shepherd. 50 mazes and labyrinths in all–classical, solid, ripple, and more–in one great volume. Perfect inexpensive puzzler for clever youngsters. Full solutions. 112pp. 8⅛ x 11. 22951-3

PIANO TUNING, J. Cree Fischer. Clearest, best book for beginner, amateur. Simple repairs, raising dropped notes, tuning by easy method of flattened fifths. No previous skills needed. 4 illustrations. 201pp. 5⅜ x 8½. 23267-0

HINTS TO SINGERS, Lillian Nordica. Selecting the right teacher, developing confidence, overcoming stage fright, and many other important skills receive thoughtful discussion in this indispensible guide, written by a world-famous diva of four decades' experience. 96pp. 5⅜ x 8½. 40094-8

THE COMPLETE NONSENSE OF EDWARD LEAR, Edward Lear. All nonsense limericks, zany alphabets, Owl and Pussycat, songs, nonsense botany, etc., illustrated by Lear. Total of 320pp. 5⅜ x 8½. (Available in U.S. only.) 20167-8

VICTORIAN PARLOUR POETRY: An Annotated Anthology, Michael R. Turner. 117 gems by Longfellow, Tennyson, Browning, many lesser-known poets. "The Village Blacksmith," "Curfew Must Not Ring Tonight," "Only a Baby Small," dozens more, often difficult to find elsewhere. Index of poets, titles, first lines. xxiii + 325pp. 5⅜ x 8¼. 27044-0

DUBLINERS, James Joyce. Fifteen stories offer vivid, tightly focused observations of the lives of Dublin's poorer classes. At least one, "The Dead," is considered a masterpiece. Reprinted complete and unabridged from standard edition. 160pp. 5³⁄₁₆ x 8¼. 26870-5

GREAT WEIRD TALES: 14 Stories by Lovecraft, Blackwood, Machen and Others, S. T. Joshi (ed.). 14 spellbinding tales, including "The Sin Eater," by Fiona McLeod, "The Eye Above the Mantel," by Frank Belknap Long, as well as renowned works by R. H. Barlow, Lord Dunsany, Arthur Machen, W. C. Morrow and eight other masters of the genre. 256pp. 5⅜ x 8½. (Available in U.S. only.) 40436-6

THE BOOK OF THE SACRED MAGIC OF ABRAMELIN THE MAGE, translated by S. MacGregor Mathers. Medieval manuscript of ceremonial magic. Basic document in Aleister Crowley, Golden Dawn groups. 268pp. 5⅜ x 8½. 23211-5

NEW RUSSIAN-ENGLISH AND ENGLISH-RUSSIAN DICTIONARY, M. A. O'Brien. This is a remarkably handy Russian dictionary, containing a surprising amount of information, including over 70,000 entries. 366pp. 4½ x 6⅛. 20208-9

HISTORIC HOMES OF THE AMERICAN PRESIDENTS, Second, Revised Edition, Irvin Haas. A traveler's guide to American Presidential homes, most open to the public, depicting and describing homes occupied by every American President from George Washington to George Bush. With visiting hours, admission charges, travel routes. 175 photographs. Index. 160pp. 8¼ x 11. 26751-2

NEW YORK IN THE FORTIES, Andreas Feininger. 162 brilliant photographs by the well-known photographer, formerly with *Life* magazine. Commuters, shoppers, Times Square at night, much else from city at its peak. Captions by John von Hartz. 181pp. 9¼ x 10¾. 23585-8

INDIAN SIGN LANGUAGE, William Tomkins. Over 525 signs developed by Sioux and other tribes. Written instructions and diagrams. Also 290 pictographs. 111pp. 6⅛ x 9¼. 22029-X

ANATOMY: A Complete Guide for Artists, Joseph Sheppard. A master of figure drawing shows artists how to render human anatomy convincingly. Over 460 illustrations. 224pp. 8⅜ x 11¼. 27279-6

MEDIEVAL CALLIGRAPHY: Its History and Technique, Marc Drogin. Spirited history, comprehensive instruction manual covers 13 styles (ca. 4th century through 15th). Excellent photographs; directions for duplicating medieval techniques with modern tools. 224pp. 8⅜ x 11¼. 26142-5

DRIED FLOWERS: How to Prepare Them, Sarah Whitlock and Martha Rankin. Complete instructions on how to use silica gel, meal and borax, perlite aggregate, sand and borax, glycerine and water to create attractive permanent flower arrangements. 12 illustrations. 32pp. 5⅜ x 8½. 21802-3

EASY-TO-MAKE BIRD FEEDERS FOR WOODWORKERS, Scott D. Campbell. Detailed, simple-to-use guide for designing, constructing, caring for and using feeders. Text, illustrations for 12 classic and contemporary designs. 96pp. 5⅜ x 8½. 25847-5

SCOTTISH WONDER TALES FROM MYTH AND LEGEND, Donald A. Mackenzie. 16 lively tales tell of giants rumbling down mountainsides, of a magic wand that turns stone pillars into warriors, of gods and goddesses, evil hags, powerful forces and more. 240pp. 5⅜ x 8½. 29677-6

THE HISTORY OF UNDERCLOTHES, C. Willett Cunnington and Phyllis Cunnington. Fascinating, well-documented survey covering six centuries of English undergarments, enhanced with over 100 illustrations: 12th-century laced-up bodice, footed long drawers (1795), 19th-century bustles, 19th-century corsets for men, Victorian "bust improvers," much more. 272pp. 5⅝ x 8¼. 27124-2

ARTS AND CRAFTS FURNITURE: The Complete Brooks Catalog of 1912, Brooks Manufacturing Co. Photos and detailed descriptions of more than 150 now very collectible furniture designs from the Arts and Crafts movement depict davenports, settees, buffets, desks, tables, chairs, bedsteads, dressers and more, all built of solid, quarter-sawed oak. Invaluable for students and enthusiasts of antiques, Americana and the decorative arts. 80pp. 6½ x 9¼. 27471-3

WILBUR AND ORVILLE: A Biography of the Wright Brothers, Fred Howard. Definitive, crisply written study tells the full story of the brothers' lives and work. A vividly written biography, unparalleled in scope and color, that also captures the spirit of an extraordinary era. 560pp. 6⅛ x 9¼. 40297-5

THE ARTS OF THE SAILOR: Knotting, Splicing and Ropework, Hervey Garrett Smith. Indispensable shipboard reference covers tools, basic knots and useful hitches; handsewing and canvas work, more. Over 100 illustrations. Delightful reading for sea lovers. 256pp. 5⅜ x 8½. 26440-8

FRANK LLOYD WRIGHT'S FALLINGWATER: The House and Its History, Second, Revised Edition, Donald Hoffmann. A total revision–both in text and illustrations–of the standard document on Fallingwater, the boldest, most personal architectural statement of Wright's mature years, updated with valuable new material from the recently opened Frank Lloyd Wright Archives. "Fascinating"–*The New York Times.* 116 illustrations. 128pp. 9¼ x 10¾. 27430-6

PHOTOGRAPHIC SKETCHBOOK OF THE CIVIL WAR, Alexander Gardner. 100 photos taken on field during the Civil War. Famous shots of Manassas Harper's Ferry, Lincoln, Richmond, slave pens, etc. 244pp. 10⅝ x 8¼. 22731-6

FIVE ACRES AND INDEPENDENCE, Maurice G. Kains. Great back-to-the-land classic explains basics of self-sufficient farming. The one book to get. 95 illustrations. 397pp. 5⅜ x 8½. 20974-1

SONGS OF EASTERN BIRDS, Dr. Donald J. Borror. Songs and calls of 60 species most common to eastern U.S.: warblers, woodpeckers, flycatchers, thrushes, larks, many more in high-quality recording. Cassette and manual 99912-2

A MODERN HERBAL, Margaret Grieve. Much the fullest, most exact, most useful compilation of herbal material. Gigantic alphabetical encyclopedia, from aconite to zedoary, gives botanical information, medical properties, folklore, economic uses, much else. Indispensable to serious reader. 161 illustrations. 888pp. 6½ x 9¼. 2-vol. set. (Available in U.S. only.) Vol. I: 22798-7
Vol. II: 22799-5

HIDDEN TREASURE MAZE BOOK, Dave Phillips. Solve 34 challenging mazes accompanied by heroic tales of adventure. Evil dragons, people-eating plants, blood-thirsty giants, many more dangerous adversaries lurk at every twist and turn. 34 mazes, stories, solutions. 48pp. 8¼ x 11. 24566-7

LETTERS OF W. A. MOZART, Wolfgang A. Mozart. Remarkable letters show bawdy wit, humor, imagination, musical insights, contemporary musical world; includes some letters from Leopold Mozart. 276pp. 5⅜ x 8½. 22859-2

BASIC PRINCIPLES OF CLASSICAL BALLET, Agrippina Vaganova. Great Russian theoretician, teacher explains methods for teaching classical ballet. 118 illustrations. 175pp. 5⅜ x 8½. 22036-2

THE JUMPING FROG, Mark Twain. Revenge edition. The original story of The Celebrated Jumping Frog of Calaveras County, a hapless French translation, and Twain's hilarious "retranslation" from the French. 12 illustrations. 66pp. 5⅜ x 8½. 22686-7

BEST REMEMBERED POEMS, Martin Gardner (ed.). The 126 poems in this superb collection of 19th- and 20th-century British and American verse range from Shelley's "To a Skylark" to the impassioned "Renascence" of Edna St. Vincent Millay and to Edward Lear's whimsical "The Owl and the Pussycat." 224pp. 5⅜ x 8½. 27165-X

COMPLETE SONNETS, William Shakespeare. Over 150 exquisite poems deal with love, friendship, the tyranny of time, beauty's evanescence, death and other themes in language of remarkable power, precision and beauty. Glossary of archaic terms. 80pp. 5$^{3}/_{16}$ x 8¼. 26686-9

THE BATTLES THAT CHANGED HISTORY, Fletcher Pratt. Eminent historian profiles 16 crucial conflicts, ancient to modern, that changed the course of civilization. 352pp. 5⅜ x 8½. 41129-X

THE WIT AND HUMOR OF OSCAR WILDE, Alvin Redman (ed.). More than 1,000 ripostes, paradoxes, wisecracks: Work is the curse of the drinking classes; I can resist everything except temptation; etc. 258pp. 5⅜ x 8½. 20602-5

SHAKESPEARE LEXICON AND QUOTATION DICTIONARY, Alexander Schmidt. Full definitions, locations, shades of meaning in every word in plays and poems. More than 50,000 exact quotations. 1,485pp. 6½ x 9¼. 2-vol. set.
Vol. 1: 22726-X
Vol. 2: 22727-8

SELECTED POEMS, Emily Dickinson. Over 100 best-known, best-loved poems by one of America's foremost poets, reprinted from authoritative early editions. No comparable edition at this price. Index of first lines. 64pp. 5³⁄₁₆ x 8¼. 26466-1

THE INSIDIOUS DR. FU-MANCHU, Sax Rohmer. The first of the popular mystery series introduces a pair of English detectives to their archnemesis, the diabolical Dr. Fu-Manchu. Flavorful atmosphere, fast-paced action, and colorful characters enliven this classic of the genre. 208pp. 5³⁄₁₆ x 8¼. 29898-1

THE MALLEUS MALEFICARUM OF KRAMER AND SPRENGER, translated by Montague Summers. Full text of most important witchhunter's "bible," used by both Catholics and Protestants. 278pp. 6⅝ x 10. 22802-9

SPANISH STORIES/CUENTOS ESPAÑOLES: A Dual-Language Book, Angel Flores (ed.). Unique format offers 13 great stories in Spanish by Cervantes, Borges, others. Faithful English translations on facing pages. 352pp. 5⅜ x 8½. 25399-6

GARDEN CITY, LONG ISLAND, IN EARLY PHOTOGRAPHS, 1869–1919, Mildred H. Smith. Handsome treasury of 118 vintage pictures, accompanied by carefully researched captions, document the Garden City Hotel fire (1899), the Vanderbilt Cup Race (1908), the first airmail flight departing from the Nassau Boulevard Aerodrome (1911), and much more. 96pp. 8⅞ x 11¾. 40669-5

OLD QUEENS, N.Y., IN EARLY PHOTOGRAPHS, Vincent F. Seyfried and William Asadorian. Over 160 rare photographs of Maspeth, Jamaica, Jackson Heights, and other areas. Vintage views of DeWitt Clinton mansion, 1939 World's Fair and more. Captions. 192pp. 8⅞ x 11. 26358-4

CAPTURED BY THE INDIANS: 15 Firsthand Accounts, 1750-1870, Frederick Drimmer. Astounding true historical accounts of grisly torture, bloody conflicts, relentless pursuits, miraculous escapes and more, by people who lived to tell the tale. 384pp. 5⅜ x 8½. 24901-8

THE WORLD'S GREAT SPEECHES (Fourth Enlarged Edition), Lewis Copeland, Lawrence W. Lamm, and Stephen J. McKenna. Nearly 300 speeches provide public speakers with a wealth of updated quotes and inspiration–from Pericles' funeral oration and William Jennings Bryan's "Cross of Gold Speech" to Malcolm X's powerful words on the Black Revolution and Earl of Spenser's tribute to his sister, Diana, Princess of Wales. 944pp. 5⅜ x 8⅜. 40903-1

THE BOOK OF THE SWORD, Sir Richard F. Burton. Great Victorian scholar/adventurer's eloquent, erudite history of the "queen of weapons"–from prehistory to early Roman Empire. Evolution and development of early swords, variations (sabre, broadsword, cutlass, scimitar, etc.), much more. 336pp. 6⅛ x 9¼.
25434-8

CATALOG OF DOVER BOOKS

THE STORY OF THE TITANIC AS TOLD BY ITS SURVIVORS, Jack Winocour (ed.). What it was really like. Panic, despair, shocking inefficiency, and a little heroism. More thrilling than any fictional account. 26 illustrations. 320pp. 5⅜ x 8½. 20610-6

FAIRY AND FOLK TALES OF THE IRISH PEASANTRY, William Butler Yeats (ed.). Treasury of 64 tales from the twilight world of Celtic myth and legend: "The Soul Cages," "The Kildare Pooka," "King O'Toole and his Goose," many more. Introduction and Notes by W. B. Yeats. 352pp. 5⅜ x 8½. 26941-8

BUDDHIST MAHAYANA TEXTS, E. B. Cowell and others (eds.). Superb, accurate translations of basic documents in Mahayana Buddhism, highly important in history of religions. The Buddha-karita of Asvaghosha, Larger Sukhavativyuha, more. 448pp. 5⅜ x 8½. 25552-2

ONE TWO THREE . . . INFINITY: Facts and Speculations of Science, George Gamow. Great physicist's fascinating, readable overview of contemporary science: number theory, relativity, fourth dimension, entropy, genes, atomic structure, much more. 128 illustrations. Index. 352pp. 5⅜ x 8½. 25664-2

EXPERIMENTATION AND MEASUREMENT, W. J. Youden. Introductory manual explains laws of measurement in simple terms and offers tips for achieving accuracy and minimizing errors. Mathematics of measurement, use of instruments, experimenting with machines. 1994 edition. Foreword. Preface. Introduction. Epilogue. Selected Readings. Glossary. Index. Tables and figures. 128pp. 5⅜ x 8½. 40451-X

DALÍ ON MODERN ART: The Cuckolds of Antiquated Modern Art, Salvador Dalí. Influential painter skewers modern art and its practitioners. Outrageous evaluations of Picasso, Cézanne, Turner, more. 15 renderings of paintings discussed. 44 calligraphic decorations by Dalí. 96pp. 5⅜ x 8½. (Available in U.S. only.) 29220-7

ANTIQUE PLAYING CARDS: A Pictorial History, Henry René D'Allemagne. Over 900 elaborate, decorative images from rare playing cards (14th–20th centuries): Bacchus, death, dancing dogs, hunting scenes, royal coats of arms, players cheating, much more. 96pp. 9¼ x 12¼. 29265-7

MAKING FURNITURE MASTERPIECES: 30 Projects with Measured Drawings, Franklin H. Gottshall. Step-by-step instructions, illustrations for constructing handsome, useful pieces, among them a Sheraton desk, Chippendale chair, Spanish desk, Queen Anne table and a William and Mary dressing mirror. 224pp. 8⅛ x 11¼. 29338-6

THE FOSSIL BOOK: A Record of Prehistoric Life, Patricia V. Rich et al. Profusely illustrated definitive guide covers everything from single-celled organisms and dinosaurs to birds and mammals and the interplay between climate and man. Over 1,500 illustrations. 760pp. 7½ x 10⅛. 29371-8